LOOK FOR THE GOOD AND YOU'LL FIND GOD

Also by Echo Bodine

Dear Echo
Echoes of the Soul
The Gift
Hands That Heal
The Key
My Big Book of Healing
Relax, It's Only a Ghost
A Still, Small Voice

LOOK FOR THE GOOD AND YOU'LL FIND GOD

The Spiritual Journey of a Psychic and Healer

ECHO BODINE

New World Library
Novato, California

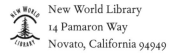

New World Library
14 Pamaron Way
Novato, California 94949

The author's experiences used as examples throughout this book are true, although
identifying details of some of the people portrayed, such as name and location,
have been changed to protect the privacy of others.

Chapter 14, "Journey to the Other Side," originally appeared in a slightly altered
form in *Echoes of the Soul* © 1999 by Echo Bodine.

Edited by Yvette Bozzini
Text design by Tona Pearce Myers

Library of Congress Cataloging-in-Publication Data
Bodine, Echo L.
  Look for the good and you'll find God : the spiritual journey of a psychic and
healer / Echo Bodine.
    p. cm.
ISBN 978-1-57731-597-1 (pbk. : alk. paper)
1. Bodine, Echo L. 2. Psychics—Biography. 3. Spiritual biography.
4. Spiritual healing. I. Title.
BF1027.B55A3 2008
133.8092—dc22[B]   2008031049

First printing, November 2008
ISBN 978-1-57731-597-1
Printed in the United States on 50% postconsumer-waste recycled paper

 New World Library is a proud member of the Green Press Initiative.

10 9 8 7 6 5 4 3 2 1

To Hap and Parker, two of God's angels

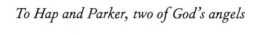

Contents

PART TWO

Living and Growing Spiritually

PART THREE

Life Today

PART ONE

Learning the Truth
about God

EVER SINCE I WAS A LITTLE GIRL, I've known that I came here to serve God and to serve people. My journey toward understanding my path has been anything but boring. I've had some amazing experiences that have shown me some very important truths about God:

God is not the enemy, is not something to be feared, does not delight in our misery. God wants to help us as much as possible. God has lots of helpers, is very creative, and *definitely* has a sense of humor.

I didn't learn these things by reading books or going to church, though I tried those things first. I studied religion in college, trying to understand what God was all about, but all this did was give me head knowledge. I still didn't feel like I was getting to the *truth* about God.

This book is about the journey I've been on since I was a young girl trying to figure things out. Who is this God I'm working for? What does He/She* want me to do? How do I do it?

In my work as a spiritual teacher, I've found that my students

---

* When I was younger, I always thought of God as male. But once I started meditating, I began to hear the voice of God, and sometimes it was a woman's voice. Since then, I've come to understand that God is a perfect balance of male and female energy. In this book, I refer to God sometimes as "He," sometimes as "She," and sometimes as "He/She."

enjoy learning from real-life stories. That's what I've put together for you — the real, and really amazing, experiences that have taught me what I know and brought me to where I am today. (I've compiled photos for this book on my website, www.echobodine.com, so that you can see some of the people in the stories.) Grab a cup of tea, put your feet up, and let me take you on a journey.

I'd like you to get yourself a brand-new journal to bring along on this journey. At the ends of most chapters I suggest some activities that I'd like you to participate in, as well as some topics to think about. Reading and writing, you'll learn a lot about yourself and more than a little about God. Before you know it, you'll be looking for the good — and finding it — in all of *your* amazing experiences.

CHAPTER ONE

My Childhood Relationship with God

ALBERT EINSTEIN IS WIDELY QUOTED as having said, "I want to know God's thoughts. The rest are details." I'm no Einstein, but that's exactly how I've always felt. For as long as I can remember, I've had a deep yearning to *know* God — and hearing Bible stories in Sunday school did not meet that need.

I grew up the oldest of four kids. Both of my parents were alcoholics, which made life unpredictable and scary. I was taught at an early age to always say my prayers at bedtime, so I did. I used to pray that my parents would quit drinking and for God to break all the whiskey bottles in the world. When this didn't happen, I got discouraged with praying. What was the point of prayers if they weren't answered?

My father's mother was a very religious woman and a member of the Women's Christian Temperance Movement. She talked about hell a lot, saying that's where drunks went when they died. She made God sound so scary. *This* was the guy I was supposed to be praying to every night? In spite of what Grandma said, and even though my prayers were unanswered, I still had a desire to know the real God. I wanted the truth and somehow *knew* there was a whole other story than the one I was hearing.

I remember my parents taking us to see *Fiddler on the Roof*. I was deeply affected by the main male character, who would go outside and talk to God all the time. I felt a yearning to be just like him, no matter how long it took.

I went from feeling discouraged to being mad at God for not answering my prayers. I decided to pray to Peter Pan instead. I figured if nothing else, he might come and take us to never-never land. Then I wouldn't care if God didn't break all the whiskey bottles. Peter never did show up, so I went back to saying my prayers at night, pleading my case to God.

Thankfully, when I was fourteen, my prayers were answered and my parents got into recovery. Life took a wonderful turn, and I felt like we were finally becoming a *normal* family. Mom and Dad both got on a spiritual path and taught me everything they were learning. I was like a person who had been in the desert for years; I soaked up everything they could give me. They would tell us really cool stories about God that they had heard at meetings, and this just made me want to know this guy even more. My father was an avid reader, and I would read his spiritual books, such as Emmet Fox's *Sermon on the Mount* and books by Norman Vincent Peale and Catherine Ponder, when he finished them. I could not quench the thirst I felt and knew I had to go even deeper, although I didn't know what that meant.

By the time I was seventeen, life was going very well. We all seemed to be healing from the previous years and were getting on with our lives. I was in my last year of high school and got accepted to the University of Minnesota. I was looking forward to becoming a social worker, a mortician, or a minister — a strange combination of interests, I know. But I felt drawn to helping people with their pain, working with the deceased, and helping people know God.

Whenever I tried to pick one career, my inner voice would tell me, "Wait." Every day I asked God to show me what His will was for my life. In the fall of 1965, I got my answer — and I wasn't at all happy about it!

CHAPTER TWO

Discovering My Spiritual Gifts

ONE NIGHT WHILE MY FAMILY WAS SITTING around the dinner table, chatting about the day, one of my brothers went downstairs to practice his drums. He was just learning to play and usually sounded kind of clanky.

After about a minute of his playing, something changed. The music began to sound really nice — smooth and professional. My parents, my sister, and my other brother all stopped talking and listened. A few minutes later, my brother came flying up the stairs. He was visibly shaken and kept asking us if we'd heard the music. We all said we had, and before we could ask him how he'd done it, he blurted out that a "white figure" had floated through the door, moved across the room, put his hands on top of my brother's, and played that really nice music. My brother said he'd tried to drop his sticks but couldn't. He also said that even though he'd had his eyes closed, he could still see this "man" playing the music through his hands.

After a few minutes, the ghostly figure had floated back across the room and out the closed door. That's when my brother dropped his sticks and came running upstairs. He was very upset and said he was never going to play his drums again.

My mother was in a prayer group at the time, and one of the women there had mentioned going to see a medium in St. Paul. Mom immediately called the woman and asked for the name and number of the medium.

When Mom called the medium and introduced herself, the medium replied, "Yes, Mrs. Bodine. I've been expecting your call." Mom told her what had happened, and the woman said the white figure was my brother's guardian angel. The angel was named Dr. Fitzgerald, and when he was living on earth, he'd been a drummer.

The medium told Mom that this had happened for a reason and that she needed to see Mom and her oldest daughter (me) for a psychic reading. She also said that Mom and her children were born with some very unusual gifts. My mother hung up the phone, telling the medium that she would call her back but that she needed time to process all this information.

When Mom told us what the medium had said, I took no comfort in the explanation that my brother had a guardian angel who used to play the drums. All I could think about was, What if I had a guardian angel who wanted to get my attention? What might it do? That night, I slept with my lights on — and they stayed on for the next two years!

Mom called the medium back the next day and set up an appointment for us. We were so curious to know what she meant by "unusual gifts" and why she'd been "expecting" our call. We had our appointment about a week later, and Mom and I freaked each other out on the drive over to St. Paul. We had *no* idea what to expect.

Mrs. Olson was an absolute sweetheart. A petite woman from

England, she had an adorable accent. Mom went in for her session first, while I sat in the living room watching TV with Mr. Olson. I was so young and naive. Seventeen and a senior in high school, I couldn't imagine what this woman could possibly have to tell me. As far as I was concerned, my life was already all planned out. I was going to attend the University of Minnesota, get a career, get married, and have a bunch of kids.

When Mrs. Olson called me into her office, I was very nervous. There was a glass of water by the chair I was sitting in, and when I reached for it to take a drink, she told me not to touch it because it was "for the spirits." What was she talking about? The whole time she was channeling a message to me, I kept an eye on the glass, wondering if the water was going to magically disappear.

Mrs. Olson had quite a bit to tell me — and nothing that I wanted to hear. She said I was born with all four of the psychic abilities and that someday I would be a world-renowned psychic. She said I would write many books, be on radio and TV, and teach others how to develop their abilities. She also said that I was born with the gift of healing and would be famous for that as well. Mrs. Olson talked about my past lives and told me that I was one of the original writers of the Mystery Schools. In a very significant past life, she said, my name was Ruth. She said she couldn't tell me who Ruth had been but that when it was important, I would find out and it would help me understand my purpose for this lifetime. (She added that this was not the Ruth of the Old Testament.)

Nothing, and I mean *nothing*, this woman said fit me, as far as I could see. I told her I had none of these abilities and no idea what she was talking about. I told her that I wasn't trying to be disrespectful but that I didn't *want* psychic abilities or the gift of healing. I was going to go to college and maybe be a social worker. I was going to have a nice, normal life. Her response was that I could have a normal life in my next life, not this one. Past lives? My next life?

I asked Mrs. Olson about a husband and children, and she said I would marry later in life and that there was a question mark above my head about children. She also said that my father was at home with a migraine headache, which was true. When I got home, she said I should lay white hankies on his head, put my hands on top of them, and ask God to work through me to heal the headache. She told me I'd had the ability to do this my whole life but had grown accustomed to it. Once I understood the gift, I would recognize that I had it.

The whole way home, I asked my mom, "Why me? Why do I have this stuff?" Mrs. Olson had told my mom that she and my brothers and sister all had the gifts as well and that we'd each do different things with them over time.

When we got home, I told Dad what Mrs. Olson had said about his migraine and asked if I could give her instructions a try. I got out some handkerchiefs and carefully placed them on his head. Then I stood back, not sure what my hands were going to do. When I placed them gently on top of the hankies, my hands immediately heated up, like little heating pads, and trembled. I stiffened them up to make the movement stop, and it did, until I relaxed my hands, when the jerking started again. After about five minutes, my hands cooled off, and Dad said, "Well, I'll be damned if my headache isn't gone."

Seventeen years old. Shy. Naive. Barely any feeling of self-worth. I'd suffered from depression since I was a kid. None of this made any sense to me, so I figured Mrs. Olson was wrong. But as little as I understood any of it, *intuitively* it felt right.

A few weeks later, my mom got a call from a woman named Birdie Torgeson. She said she was a spiritualist minister in the Twin

Cities and that her spirit guides had given her the names of eight people in the area whom she was supposed to help develop their psychic abilities. Mom's name — and mine — were on the list.

A woman we had never met calls us out of the blue to tell us her spirit guides told her to teach us to develop our abilities! All I could think was, "What in God's name is going on?" And speaking of God, what did *He* think of all this? Did He endorse it? Was He behind it? Or was this all from the dark side, like some of my friends were saying?

Every night I prayed for clarification. Was this something He wanted me to do? Was this His will? What about my will? What about college, marriage, and kids? Why was life going in this direction?

Mom and I did attend the psychic development classes for about a year and learned a great deal about spirituality and psychic abilities. Even so, my mind was all over the place trying to figure it all out. Unfortunately, no answers came. Well, none that I could see.

CHAPTER THREE

A Dark Period

MRS. OLSON TOLD ME that I came into this lifetime with many issues to work out. I would experience most of this turmoil early in life, she said, and then later use the wisdom I had gained to help others. In retrospect, the summer after my graduation from high school kicked off a six-year period that was indeed filled with turmoil and lessons.

During this time, I had my heart broken by someone I thought I was really in love with. Because of this experience, I started college with a chip on my shoulder. As I've described, my family was healing from the pain alcoholism had earlier caused us. We were all much better on the outside but had lots of unresolved pain on the inside. My pain became more and more apparent after the breakup. I was also still hoping that Mrs. Olson was wrong about my path in life. I just wanted to meet Mr. Right and live happily ever after.

During my first quarter at college, I was asked to the homecoming dance by a very handsome young biology major. I was sure he was going to be my Mr. Right. The night of the dance, we went out to dinner with another couple, and my date asked me what I'd like to drink. (He'd brought along a fake ID for me.) In that split second, my life changed.

I had made a pact with my brother when we were kids that we were never going to drink. Our pediatrician had told our mother that the odds of at least two of us four kids becoming alcoholic were very high. I loathed alcohol, but this was (possibly) Mr. Right asking me to drink. The boy who'd broken my heart had split up with me because I wasn't a "party girl." I didn't want that to happen again, so I looked at my date and told him I'd have whatever he was having.

To this day, I don't remember a thing about what happened after that first drink. I had a total blackout that night — and just about every subsequent time I drank. It was pretty obvious from that first night that I was not a light social drinker.

I never drank in moderation. I drank hard liquor and drank it fast because I couldn't wait to reach the point of being oblivious to the pain I was feeling inside. When I got there, the insecurities that plagued me and the depression that was always with me went away. I found that I felt beautiful, smart, and sexy when I drank. So I drank.

I continued to date this potential Mr. Right for almost a year. When he transferred to another college, we drifted apart, and I met another young man. I was immediately attracted to this new man for all the wrong reasons. Yes, he was smart and good-looking, but he was also cool and aloof and acted like he couldn't care less about me. He was the ultimate challenge, and I was determined to make him mine. When he asked me to marry him, I was on cloud nine.

We had many differences, but they didn't seem to matter. Winning his love validated me as a person, so I tried not to think about all that separated us. He was Jewish; I was Christian. He hated alcoholics, and I was becoming one. My psychic abilities were growing, and he didn't believe in any of it. I had a relationship with God, and he didn't.

When I was a sophomore, I became pregnant by this wonderful man who just wasn't the best fit for me. I already had a great deal of shame and guilt about having sex before marriage. Now I was pregnant. Because of my shame, I didn't know if I could turn to God for help and guidance. I felt awful about who I had become and assumed God felt the same way. I literally cried and prayed for three days, pleading for answers. In the end, I knew that I needed to give birth to my child and place him for adoption, even though my boyfriend felt certain that we should get married and keep our baby. He and I received some premarital counseling, and the counselor did not think I was ready to become a wife and mother. In addition, my boyfriend was about to join the army.

It was so odd to have what I thought I wanted so badly — a husband and child — placed right in front of me and still know that this was not my path. I knew intuitively that God was telling me to trust that there was another road for all three of us. No matter how much I pleaded with God for a different answer, I would always get the same sense that I was not supposed to go down the road of what I thought I wanted.

This was not easy, and I struggled. It was tremendously difficult to want what I wanted *and* know I should not take it.

Ultimately, I went to California, stayed with family friends while I went through my pregnancy, and then relinquished my son. When I came back from California, I went deeper into depression and began drinking again to stop the pain of my loss. My boyfriend and I stopped seeing each other at the insistence of my parents, but we eventually got back together for a few more years.

When I was younger and went through bad bouts of depression, my mom taught me to focus on others and on how I could be helpful to them. This always seemed to help lift the dark cloud of hopelessness and despair (for a while). I asked God to show me how I could turn this experience into something good. I truly felt that if I didn't find something positive in having placed my son for adoption, I would lose my mind.

One day, shortly after that prayer, I felt directed to go home for lunch after my morning shift as a waitress. I turned on the television while eating and saw a minister from Lutheran Social Services. He was talking about a program they had for unwed mothers who were trying to adjust to life with or without their babies. I couldn't believe what I was hearing. I called the number on the screen and spoke to the woman in charge of the program. She invited me to their next meeting.

Our group was dedicated to reaching out to the teenage community and to preventing as many unwed pregnancies as we could. We began speaking at high schools and church camps. We traveled a five-state area, simply sharing our stories. We wanted the kids to see that teen pregnancy didn't just happen to the girl on the wrong side of the tracks, or to the girl who slept around; it could happen to anyone having sex without birth control, and even sometimes with birth control. We talked to so many young men and women who didn't have a clue about responsible sex. For example, one girl said that her boyfriend had told her that if she ate a lot of peanut butter just before having sex, she wouldn't get pregnant.

This program was a blessing for all of us who had gone through unwanted pregnancies. We found a way to turn our scars into stars. It felt fantastic to help other young people while healing ourselves.

WILL THE REAL GOD PLEASE STAND UP?

As a kid, I remember hearing adults say that bad things happened to people because God made them happen. There's so much in the Bible about the wrath of God, it's no wonder most of us aren't sure what to think when bad things happen to us.

The Old Testament is full of horror stories about God's vengeance. Then Jesus comes along in the New Testament and tries to convince us that God loves us unconditionally. What are we supposed to believe?

During this dark time in my life, I wondered why He hadn't prevented it. Why did I have to go through all this hard stuff? Why did I have to give up a baby I wanted to keep? Why did I have to grow up so much faster than my friends? I didn't see any of it as what I was doing to myself; all of it was what God was doing to me.

This put me at odds with God. I wanted to reach out to Him but was afraid to. This was partly because of the guilt I felt and partly just plain fear of what else I might have to go through. Every time something went wrong in my life, from a parking ticket to my unplanned pregnancy, I assumed it was God's way of punishing me for the way I was living. I look back on those days and shudder. It was such a lonely time.

FOR YOU TO THINK ABOUT

How Is Your Relationship with God?

Does any of this ring true for you? Do you see God as a kind and loving "good guy" or as a stern and angry "bad guy?" Do you worry about being punished?

Get these thoughts and feelings out in your journal. You're not going to hurt God's feelings by writing this all out! Do you think God is responsible for all the crummy things happening in the world? Are you able to turn to God in times of need, or do you avoid Him for fear of ticking Him off even more?

Make a list of all the things that you are resentful of God about — the personal things and the world events that you see as "acts of God."

Then write a letter to God. Describe every big and little thing that has made you mad at, scared of, or resentful of Him. Get it all off your chest. This is the only way your relationship with God can improve. Don't worry about God smiting you for telling your truth. He has heard it all before.

When you're done with the list and the letter, go back over them. Honestly and objectively look for any good that came out of the "bad." Look for lessons learned, positive change, and growth in yourself and in others.

This may take time and a bit of thought. Many conflicting feelings may come up for you. Keep at it.

This exercise is not about finding the silver lining in every cloud. It's about enlarging your vision and deepening your perspective. Primarily, it's about giving you the relationship with God that you deserve. When we are able to face and share all our fears and feelings, we can have a real, mature relationship, with ourselves — and with God.

CHAPTER FOUR

Angels among Us

BY THE TIME I WAS TWENTY-FOUR, my life was out of control. I wanted to get on my true path, but the thought of living without my liquid courage terrified me. I would pray and ask God for help to quit but then go off on one of my binges. Over and over I turned my back on the help He was trying to give me.

Looking back, I see that this help came in two different forms that year. The first was when I was rear-ended by a drunk driver and ended up in the hospital for ten days, in traction. My neck, arms, shoulders, and back were injured, and I was in constant pain. I had three different doctors doling out pain pills like human PEZ dispensers. Before long, I was hooked on all of it — Valium to relax my muscles, Talwin and Fiorinal for headaches, Codeine for general pain, and Percodan for back pain. It wasn't long before I discovered how much more effective all these pills were if I washed them down with alcohol. I was a mess.

I managed to get myself up for work every day, but I was usu- ally late. At the time I was working as executive secretary for the vice president of a car dealership. My boss pressured me to clean up my act, but I always used the excuse that I was in a lot of pain, and he'd back down for a while.

My best friend, Cheryl, and I frequented a bar called Uncle Sam's. Two or three nights a week — depending on how hungover we were — we'd hit this downtown Minneapolis spot. I was not a happy drunk. I was angry and belligerent, and I felt sorry for myself.

God's second offer of help arrived at Uncle Sam's, in the form of a man named "BT." Cher and I called him our mystery man. At least once a week, BT would turn up and buy us a round. He wasn't much of a drinker himself, nursing one Black Russian the whole night. He told us he was a fishing guide in northern Minnesota — a description that fit him about as well as it fit me. He would say nothing about his home or family. He dodged all personal questions, which is why we called him our mystery man.

One thing BT was clear about was that he was bothered by my drinking. He always called me "princess" and told me that his "ol' man" had died a drunk. I was hitting the booze just as hard as he had, BT said, and he didn't want me to die the same way. In my belligerent way, I would tell him to mind his own business and leave me alone.

I didn't really want him to go away any more than I wanted to be a drunk, or to turn my back on God. There was something so sweet, so special, about BT. It was comforting to have him around and nice to have a man care without asking for anything in return.

One night BT came down to the bar when I was in a particularly foul mood. He started in on me about drinking pop instead of booze, and I really laid into him. I told him my drinking was none of his business and to get lost — and this time he did. He stayed away from me for close to a month, and I really missed him.

Then one Saturday morning, BT telephoned. He had never called my home before. He asked if I would have dinner with him, saying he had some things he wanted to talk to me about. "I'll call you as soon as I'm done with work," he said, "and please lay off the sauce for the day." I promised I would — though I did pop a few Valium to get me through until he called back.

At 6:05 that evening, the phone rang. It wasn't BT but a frantic Cher instead. "Turn on the news," she said. When I did, I saw what she was so upset about: BT had been shot and killed that day by the police.

I immediately went into the kitchen, downed two more Valium, and proceeded to drink an entire fifth of brandy, my Christmas gift from my boss.

The week leading up to BT's funeral, I stayed stoned on prescription meds. I felt so much regret for the way I'd treated my mystery man. I wanted to take my behavior back or at least make it up to him. There was no way that I could do that now.

I was an emotional basket case on the day of the funeral, but that night, I had made a commitment to go to a dance. Ironically, it was at one of the halfway houses in town. My mother was in recovery and knew others in recovery groups, including the owner of the halfway house, which held weekly dances. He invited us both to come to the dance, and I had told him I'd be there. I popped a Valium and went.

One of the addicts who lived at the house asked me why I was so down. I told him that a dear friend of mine had died that week and that I had been to his funeral that day. He asked me who it was and I told him, "BT."

This man became agitated. "How on earth did you know *him?*" When I explained that BT was a really sweet guy who was trying to get me to quit drinking, the addict went off about BT being a notorious — and ruthless — cocaine dealer. "No, no," I insisted. "He was a fishing guide up north." The guy burst out laughing. "And I've got some swampland to sell you," he grinned.

Other residents of the house confirmed that BT was a well-known dealer and that the police had been trying to bust him for a long time. It seemed that these people had known a different man from the one I knew. BT had always treated me well, the perfect gentleman, and God spoke to me through BT. Handsome and well dressed, the BT I knew was soft-spoken and kind. It shocked me that he could be so different to them yet still be this man who had worried about my drinking and worried about me. He'd often told me he didn't want me to die a drunk, like his "ol' man" had.

I stayed stoned for the next two weeks, taking all the pills I could without overdosing. One night I had a date with a man, but I was too drunk to go out. I heard my sister talking on the phone to him, making excuses for me. I heard her say, "No, she's not drunk again. She just doesn't feel good." The next morning, February 3, 1973, I woke up in a cold sweat. Remembering her words from the night before made me feel sick. Finally, I *knew* the time had come. I had to quit.

I went to my first AA meeting terrified of living without the pills and alcohol but feeling I no longer had a choice. As we made our way into the small meeting room, lo and behold, into the room came the spirit of my dear friend BT. He had a huge smile on his face and stood behind me with his hands on my shoulders. He called me "princess" and told me he was very proud of me. He stayed for about five minutes, and when he left, I felt really happy inside. That night was the beginning of a brand-new way of life.

FOR YOU TO THINK ABOUT

Who Are the Angels in Your Life?

Reflect back on your life and look for the angels God has put on your path. Who nudged you to be a better person? Who called you on self-destructive behavior? Who made a comment that changed your life?

God speaks through all of us. We can touch people's lives without being aware of it. My students often tell me about things I've said that shifted them out of fear or that answered questions they didn't even know how to formulate. When this happens, I know that God has spoken to them through me.

Recognizing these connections to God helps us grow spiritually, so make a list of your BTs. Then think about whose BT you have been. Have you ever heard wise words coming out of your mouth and wondered where they were coming from? Has a friend ever told you later that your words or actions had been important to them in ways you hadn't imagined? And has a person many considered "bad" ever had a positive effect on you?

Write down these incidents and experiences, and you'll see angels in action.

CHAPTER FIVE

God Speaks in Mysterious Ways

MY SENSE OF SELF-WORTH was practically nonexistent by the time I quit drinking. I had a lot of fear and anxiety that needed healing. I had unresolved pain from my childhood and a truckload of guilt and shame for things I had done during my drinking days. My relationship with God was in dire need of repair. And on top of all this, I was still confused about whether my growing psychic abilities were good or bad, right or wrong. Joining AA was the best thing that ever happened to me, but when I mentioned my abilities to a few people in the program, they reacted so negatively that I decided to keep them to myself. (To clarify, it's not the policy of AA to make a judgment about anything. The people who reacted negatively were sharing their own beliefs.)

Each day, as the fog lifted a little bit more — an AA expression for when you're first sobering up — I became aware that my inner thirst to know God was back in force. The third step of the program says to turn our life and our will over to the care of God *as we understand God*, asking only for knowledge of His will for us and the power to carry that out. I struggled to understand and act on this.

One Saturday morning, while attending a meeting in which this third step was being discussed, I realized I was nervous about this "turning our life and will over to God" business. After the meeting, I stood in line at a grocery store. I stared at a bouquet of balloons by the register as my mind wandered. What would my life be like if I did turn it over to God? As my mind drifted back to my place in the line, I took note of how colorful the balloons were. I thought about how I'd loved these bright balls of color since I was a little girl.

As I walked home from the market, I asked God to give me some kind of sign that He was really on my side. I explained that I *knew* I needed to turn my life and my will over to Him but was anxious and fearful about doing it. Could He somehow let me know He wasn't mad at me? Show me that turning my will over was a good thing? "I'd really appreciate it," I prayed.

Later that afternoon, there was a knock on my door. When I said, "Who's there?" I heard one of the guys from my AA group say that he had something for me. I opened the door, and there he stood with a bouquet of balloons! He asked if it was my birthday.

"Nope," I said, with a huge smile on my face.

"That's strange," he replied, explaining that he'd been nudged intuitively to get me the bouquet and didn't know why. He asked if I had any idea.

I told him the balloons were a sign from God — and thanked him profusely for listening to that nudge.

Later that day, I sat down and wrote in my journal that I was consciously taking the step to turn my life and my will over to the care of God. I wasn't sure what to do besides share this with God. Other than having an inner sense that this was the beginning of a new journey, nothing monumental happened. Well, nothing except my balloons.

Fast-forward many years to another example of God speaking in mysterious ways:

There was a woman in one of my classes — I'll call her "Dee" — whom I always felt a certain kinship with. One Saturday morning before class started, Dee told me that she hoped to be just like me someday — teaching classes, doing healings and readings, and having the faith in God to live by her intuition, as I do. We hugged, and I thanked Dee for the compliment. Little did either of us know just how alike we already were.

A few minutes later, another student came in with flowers for me. Dee asked what the flowers were for, and I told her that it was my birthday. "It's my birthday, too!" Dee exclaimed. I asked her what year she was born, and she said 1948. "Me, too," I said. When I asked where she was born, we learned we were both natives of St. Paul.

We kept going. "What hospital?" I asked. When she replied, "Midway," I again said, "Me, too." We were shaking our heads in wonder by this point. "What time were you born?" I asked next. When Dee said, "10:05 PM," I knew that we'd been nursery mates. I was born at 9:04 PM.

We were born one hour and one minute apart, bunked in the nursery together for a week, went our separate ways for forty years, and met back up in psychic development classes. We laughed, and I smiled at the confirmation that there really are no coincidences in life.

As it turns out, Dee and I had very similar life paths. We both grew up in alcoholic families. Like me, Dee got pregnant before marriage. She didn't have the addiction problems that I've struggled with, but she's been around addiction her whole life. We both had difficult childhoods. We've both dealt with codependency issues and are both members of Al-Anon (a support organization for family and friends of alcoholics). Both of us are authors, healers, and psychics, though Dee has not made a career out of her psychic abilities.

We haven't seen each other for several years, but we always send each other birthday cards. I imagine that our souls had quite a bit to talk about while we were waiting for our bodies to be born that night in Midway Hospital, September 20, 1948.

I think that sometimes God sends a balloon — or a nursery mate! — just to remind us we aren't alone.

FOR YOU TO THINK ABOUT

Have You Experienced Any Coincidences Lately?

Have you ever heard the expression "a coincidence is God's way of remaining anonymous"?

I believe that we're frequently given signs that God is watching over us but we tend to blow these off as coincidences. Instead of doing this, ask God to show you signs that He is watching over you. Then start paying closer attention to what's going on in your life. When you experience "coincidences," write about them in your journal.

You might get an obvious sign, like my balloons, or you may slowly start to notice more everyday occurrences — a check arriving unexpectedly just when you need it, or running into a friend you've been meaning to call.

The important thing is to shift the way we think about

things, to look with fresh eyes. I want you to start realizing that you are more important than you think. Coincidences aren't random; if something is happening to you, it's because it's meant for you. In every experience, look for a sign from God, a message just for you. I think you'll soon see so many of these messages, you'll wonder how you ever could have missed them.

Pause, pay attention, and remember: look for the good, and you'll find God. Also remember that growing spiritually is an adventure. It doesn't happen overnight — and it wouldn't be half as much fun if it did.

CHAPTER SIX

Answers to Prayers

HAVE YOU EVER HEARD THE STORY about the guy sitting on top of his flooding house, praying for help? A boat comes along to rescue him, but he says no, he's waiting for God to help him. The Coast Guard arrives, and the man waves them away, saying he's waiting for God. Then a helicopter hovers overhead and — you guessed it — the man refuses to get in because he's waiting for God. When the man drowns and goes to heaven, he asks God, "Why didn't you help me?" God replies, "I sent a boat, the Coast Guard, and a helicopter. What more did you want me to do?"

It's easy to be so sure of *how* we think prayers should be answered that we miss the real deal.

As I wrote earlier, I met with a lot of resistance to coming out of the psychic closet. Some friends voiced negative (religious) opinions about my abilities. Three different friends, in fact, told me that if I decided to turn these abilities into a career, and took money for my work, they would no longer be my friends.

I prayed daily for signs about whether or not using my abilities was God's will. Just like the man on the roof, I failed to see answer after answer. I was oblivious to even a big, blinking neon sign of a reply. Here's what I mean:

During my first year in AA, I slowly made new friends. One of the women in my group asked if I'd like to have dinner with her. She had a rough way about her that I found intimidating, but I thought it would be good for me to do more socializing.

We met at a cafeteria-style steak house. When we were standing in line, waiting to order, a male spirit appeared in front of me. He told me that he had some important things that I needed to say to this woman. No way, I thought. I barely know this woman, and she scares me a bit. How could I risk letting her know I can see and communicate with dead people? I mentally told the spirit to buzz off.

As the woman and I continued down the line, the male spirit blocked my way and said it was *extremely* important that I give my friend a message. I just kept pretending I didn't see him and sent a firm telepathic message, "Go away!" Happily, by the time we got to the end of the line, the spirit had taken a hike.

We ordered our food and sat down at a table. Within seconds, the unwelcome spirit joined us. Exasperated, I took a deep breath and told my new friend that I had psychic abilities. I ignored the wide-eyed look on her face and told her that there was a male spirit determined to give her a message. Was she open to hearing what he had to say? When she nodded yes, I closed my eyes and told her everything the spirit was saying, word for word. He had a great deal to say, and it was all very personal.

When I finished channeling the message, the spirit disappeared. Nervously, I asked my friend, "Are you okay?"

At first she couldn't talk. Then she told me that just that morning, she'd told God that she was giving Him one day to prove He existed. She gave him three problems in her life and said she wanted answers to all three or she wasn't going to believe in Him anymore. What the spirit said referred to her three problems.

You'd think I'd have taken this incident as a sign, a green light telling me it was safe to go ahead and share my abilities with people. But no, I didn't get it. I remained stopped by all my internal red lights.

The next sign came on a Saturday afternoon. I was getting ready for a date, when there was a knock on the door. I opened it to find a man from one of my AA groups. He was standing with his eyes closed and said that he'd had a migraine headache for three days. When he'd asked God for help with the pain, something told him to come to my apartment.

I told him that I was born with the gift of healing but that if I got rid of his headache, he had to promise not to tell anyone.

I laid my hands on his head. For about five minutes, heat poured out of them. When they cooled off, I told the man to lie on my couch until he felt ready to leave. Then I excused myself so that I could finish getting ready. About ten minutes later, he knocked on the bathroom door to let me know his headache was gone. "Remember our deal," I said. He and I never mentioned the healing again.

Even though I was praying for guidance about whether I should let people know about my gifts, I was so stuck in my fear of rejection that I wouldn't let myself see the answers. There's a verse in the Bible (Luke 16:13) about not serving two masters. I felt I had to decide who I was going to serve. Would I serve the people who wanted me to be "normal," or would I heed my inner voice?

At the end of my first year of sobriety, I took an inventory of my life. I realized that experiences like the ones I've just described were signs from God that He wanted me to use my spiritual gifts. I was embarrassed about all the resistance I had thrown up and told Him I was sorry for being so worried about what other people would think of me. If He wanted me to use these gifts, I would.

The next night, I was on a date, and we were doubling with a couple I had met only briefly. We were all on our way to a hockey game when I got a psychic image: Ginny, the other woman in the car, had a blockage in one of the arteries leading to her heart. "I'm on a *date*," I silently pleaded to God. "These people don't know this stuff about me." I tried not to see the pictures in my mind's eye, but a vision of my hands on her heart would not go away. I looked around, watched traffic, and made small talk with my date. Still, the image remained frozen in my mind, as though someone had pressed the pause button on a TV remote.

I then remembered what I'd promised God. I knew that if I didn't stop resisting, my internal struggles would never end. So I turned around to the woman in the backseat, asked her if she was in pain, and pointed right to the area I saw around her heart. Everyone in the car went silent, but she said yes, she did have pain there. I blocked out the startled looks on everyone's faces and explained that I was born with the gift of healing and psychic abilities. I said that if she wanted, I could channel a healing. There were several awkward moments of silence in the car followed by her saying that she would be very open to receiving a healing.

Over the course of a few weeks, I channeled several healings to the blockages, and she was fine. I never went out with my date of that night again, but Ginny and I became best friends.

CHAPTER SEVEN

Thank God for the Experience

WHEN I WAS TWENTY-SIX, I was hopelessly in love with a practicing alcoholic. It wasn't a good situation, because I was just beginning my second year of recovery and should have been paying more attention to my sobriety instead of focusing on his.

The object of my affection had been in and out of treatment, in and out of jail, and in and out of more jobs than you might think possible. He was also adorable, funny, and charismatic. He had good morals and values — and looked like a million bucks in a suit.

Every time this man disappeared for a few days, he left many broken hearts in his wake. Whenever this happened, I came to expect a call from a detox facility or a jail. He was *seriously* addicted.

I'd seen so many wonderful miracles (people) in AA, I was sure there was something I could do for him. If I could just get him to meetings, he would certainly catch on to sobriety, and then we could live happily ever after!

I prayed. I gave him pamphlets. I told him about the meetings

I was going to. And all the while, I was becoming a wreck because of the toll his lies and lifestyle were taking on me.

I finally hit bottom with the relationship when he was sentenced to the workhouse *again*, for driving without a license. I prayed for guidance for the hundredth time. I knew I had to get out of the relationship but didn't know how. My head would say something sensible, and then my heart would say, "But, but, but..." Common sense was losing the debate, and I was exhausted from trying to figure it all out.

I called my dear friend Ginny, hoping to talk it all out and get back to some sanity. She made a suggestion that I thought was ridiculous: thank God every day for my experience. "You're kidding, right?" I asked. She said she wasn't and that I should try it for a few days and see what happened.

I figured that since none of my bright ideas was working, I didn't have a lot to lose. So every night when I went to bed, or during the day when I found myself trying to find a solution for "us," I thanked God for the experience. When a letter arrived from the workhouse, I thanked God some more. Then one night, when I was in bed crying about my guy's addiction, I thanked God for the pain I was in, and suddenly the pain began to lessen. It felt like a weight was being lifted off my heart and chest.

My thoughts and feelings began to change. Instead of feeling only pain and powerlessness, I began to feel gratitude for how much I was learning and growing. Instead of thinking up ways to "save" this man, I thanked God for showing me that this wasn't my job. Instead of feeling sorry for myself for loving him, I became thankful for all the good it had done me. From this perspective, what had seemed impossible was doable: I could move on. I could feel my pain — and my love — and still leave.

A simple (but not so simple at first) prayer of thanks for a difficult situation *changed* the situation. He may still have been drinking or detoxing, in jail or the workhouse, but I was in a dramatically different place. I now knew, in my head and in my heart, that no matter how much planning, praying, or plotting I did, I could not control another person's addiction.

Whenever I become preoccupied with another person's behavior, I know it's time to put the focus back on myself. I joined Al-Anon, which was a godsend. It helped me deal with the other addictive people in my life, and it taught me about surrendering my will and letting go.

FOR YOU TO THINK ABOUT

Whose Inventory Are You Taking?

Statistics show that just about everyone has an alcoholic in his or her family or a friend suffering from some form of addiction. Addiction is one of the most difficult life lessons to learn from, both for the addicts and for the people who love them. The pain of watching someone practice an addiction — while we stand by, powerless — is excruciating. But there is something you can do: know that this person is in your life for a reason. If all you're feeling right now is pain, know that you can change this when you're ready to.

For today, work on looking at the situation differently. What positives have come out of it for you? What have you gained from having this person in your life? Write your answers in your journal.

I know it can seem that no good can come out of a

relationship with an addict. But most of us hang in there for as long as we can. This is evidence that there is something — lessons, healing, personal and spiritual growth — to be gained.

Start thanking God daily for the experience of having this person in your life. Do this even if your thanks don't feel genuine at first. As awareness of the good in the situation grows in you, record it in your journal. This will help you shift the way you look at *all* the experiences in your life. Painful feelings of hopelessness and helplessness lift.

You can't change the way the addict sees things, but when you change the way *you* do, you can heal. That's what you can do, and it's the good waiting to be found in even the lousiest of situations. Thank God.

CHAPTER EIGHT

Fishes and Loaves

WHEN I'D EXPERIENCED A FEW NEW YEAR'S EVES sober, I realized that there was a gaping hole in what was available for recovering alcoholics and their families to do on that night.

One evening after an AA meeting, several of us were having coffee at a restaurant and started tossing around the idea of planning something for New Year's Eve. As I recall, there were about five of us who felt very inspired to do something. We started meeting weekly to plan an event, a huge party for alcoholics and their families to attend during the holidays.

One thing led to another, and before we knew it, we were planning two events: a twenty-four-hour one for Christmas and another twenty-four-hour event for New Year's. Our biggest challenge was getting the word out to all the AA meetings in town. Most clubhouses didn't have phone numbers, and since this was back in the mid-seventies, no one had a cell phone.

I look back now and wonder where we got the gumption to move ahead with such a big enterprise on absolutely no money.

Everything needed to be donated. We asked Al-Anon members to get involved, and before we knew it, we had both events planned. We had bands coming in for New Year's, plus speakers, games, and every-hour meetings available. We brought in some cots for people who had no place to sleep. Several groups signed up to bring in food. It came together with very little effort, and we were all excited.

Word spread fast throughout the 12-step community. People from all over volunteered their time and whatever service they could provide.

The Christmas Alcathon came off without a hitch. People were so grateful to have a place to come to. We had a huge crowd of people show up for breakfast on Christmas morning and later served several turkey dinners with all the fixings. It was a wonderful experience for all of us.

A week later, we had the New Year's Eve Alcathon and were all set to feed the same number of people we had the week before. We had no idea that *triple* the number of people would be showing up. By 11:30 on New Year's Eve, we had run out of food!

We had turkeys for dinner the next day, but they were still thawing. The sausages and pancakes we had were for breakfast. Several of us stood in a tiny kitchen trying to figure out how in the world we were going to feed all these people, and with all the stores closed. We looked at the small pan of chili cooking on the stove and knew *it* wasn't going to make a dent in the appetites of the people who kept pouring in for the celebration.

Someone commented that if we only had "a couple fish and a few loaves of bread," we could do whatever Jesus did to feed the multitudes. I remember my inner voice saying that everything was going to be just fine and to stop fretting. But without any idea of *how* this might all work out, it was hard not to worry.

Shortly after midnight, several people from AA and Al-Anon groups around town began showing up with boxes and bags of sandwiches, as well as cookies and snack bars. The kitchen was soon filled to bursting with food. We all stood there in awe, feeling incredibly grateful. It was a wonderful reminder that God loved those hungry people as much as we did — and would always take care of us.

FOR YOU TO THINK ABOUT

Everyday Miracles

Can you think of a time when God pulled a "fishes and loaves" number in your life? Or when you had the gumption to try to realize a big idea against all odds?

Many times when we try to be of service, we face unexpected roadblocks and detours. Can you think of a situation when you couldn't see an answer but then experienced a surprise solution?

Write about it. Miracles happen every day and deserve to be seen as such. When we recognize them, we get the courage to think big. We learn to do our part and then trust. We get proof that if we work hard and our goal is a good one, obstacles will be overcome, one way or another, and in their time. We feel and see our partnership with God.

CHAPTER NINE

Barber School

WHEN I WAS TWENTY-SEVEN and had a few years of sobriety under my belt, I wanted to find a fulfilling way to earn my living. My psychic and healing gifts were coming along slowly. I practiced minireadings on friends and did healings on family members when they got sick. But I didn't feel ready to "go pro" with my gifts.

I was working at this time as a receptionist/secretary at an employment agency for recovering alcoholics. My boss encouraged me to go back to school to earn a degree in chemical dependency counseling. I took his advice, but after a one-month internship at a halfway house, I knew this wasn't the work for me. I left the program before getting my degree.

One night during an AA meeting, I talked about wanting to find a career. Someone suggested I look into my heart and think about the things I loved doing. There *was* something I had always loved: fixing hair. It let me be creative, and the idea of making people look and feel good appealed to me.

One of the things I had learned about God's will in sobriety is that if something is His will for us, the pieces fall into place easily.

My job at the employment agency was perfect because I had access to various places in town where a person could apply for financial aid for school. I wound up applying to the local barber college and was accepted. The only glitch was a two-year waiting list to begin.

I asked God what I should do. This delay didn't feel right. It felt like I was meant to start school with the new spring class.

My inner voice told me to ask the owner of the college how I could begin in the spring. I went down to the school and told him I really wanted to get into school as soon as possible. He told me that the only way I would was if he got three cancellations between now and the start date. He warned me not to get my hopes up because there were two people ahead of me on the cancellation list and people rarely gave up their place on the list.

I stood up, shook his hand, and told him I was going to pray for three cancellations.

"You're gonna do what? Did you say 'pray'?"

"Yes, sir," I replied. "I'm going to pray for three cancellations — and I'll see you in the spring."

Every few weeks, my inner voice nudged me to send the owner a "thinking of you" card to remind him that I was praying. About six weeks after our meeting, he called. "You must have some great connections," he said. "I just got a third cancellation. See you soon."

But all my problems were not solved. I had to figure out how to make enough money to support myself while attending school. Two days later, the owner called me again. Would I be interested in a janitor/office job at the school? Bingo: the money I needed to live on.

I really liked school and loved cutting hair. Men were easy to work with, and it was always fun to send them off looking nice. All the while, my psychic and healing abilities were growing stronger.

My hands would heat up during a haircut if the customer needed healing. Once in a while, psychic information would pop out of my mouth if someone needed guidance. A man might come and sit in my barber chair, and as I worked on him, my hands would heat up and I'd have an urge to touch his back. The client might ask me why my hands were hot, and when I told him, he'd mention pain he'd had or an injury, and I would hold my hands to his back. One man complained of how his wife was acting, and the words "she's going through menopause" popped out of my mouth. This information threw him for a loop. I seldom told people I had these gifts unless I was guided to do so, but often I'd say something to them that they would later tell me made a big difference for them.

After graduating from the college, I was lined up to start working at a brand-new barbershop in downtown Minneapolis. Construction delays on this new shop forced me to find a temporary job. When I called the director of my school for help, he had just gotten off the phone with the shop at the University of Minnesota. They needed someone for just a few weeks. How perfect was that? Little did I know...

A few days after I started at the university barbershop, I got a call from my friend Ginny telling me her fourteen-year-old stepson had fallen eighteen feet and landed on his head. He had been flown from Nebraska to the University of Minnesota hospital, where he was in a coma with a horrible prognosis. A nurse told the family that if the boy ever came out of the coma he would remain a "vegetable," so she advised them to put him in a nursing home to save themselves time and money.

Ginny asked if I would do healings on her stepson. After getting the go-ahead from my inner voice, I started seeing him every day. The hospital was literally one block from the barbershop I was working at, so I could walk down on my lunch break and after work.

On the second day that I was channeling healing to him, I felt a presence standing behind me, though I knew I was alone in the room. Then I heard a voice say, "Please heal the speech part of my brain. I want to talk again." I slowly turned around to see who was in the room, and there, leaning up against the wall, was a spirit, or so I thought. I asked him who he was, and he said he was the soul that lived in this body and that he wanted to speak again so could I please work on the speech part of his brain. I asked him how he could be out of the body if he was its soul, and he said that souls can leave their bodies anytime they want. He also said that when he stepped out of his body, his body felt no pain, so he was stepping out often to give his body a break.

I was very surprised by this but very grateful because even though his body was in a coma, I could still communicate with him. Every day when I went to channel healing to him, his soul would come out of his body and talk to me. He told me when his head hurt or knees were in pain.

This is how I learned I could communicate directly with souls. It was a life-changing experience for me because ever since then when I've channeled a healing to someone, I've communicated with their soul.

Six weeks later, when it was time for me to leave the university barbershop and head downtown to the new shop, this young man left the hospital walking and talking on his own. The whole experience was a huge turning point for both of us, and I gained so much wisdom from it. (You can read more about this healing in my book *Echoes of the Soul*.)

The boy's soul was completely aware of everything while his physical body was in the coma. The soul was somewhat detached emotionally; it looked at the body almost the way we look at our cars. We use our cars to get us around in life, just as the soul uses the body to get around. We are in our cars but not part of our cars, which is similar to the way a soul inhabits a body. We humans are in charge of where our cars go; our souls are in charge of where our bodies go. My life and work changed forever because of this experience.

FOR YOU TO THINK ABOUT

What Are the Desires in Your Heart?

Do you have dreams that you're afraid to pursue? Does a lack of money hold you back? Do you worry about what people will say if you pursue your dreams?

When I was a senior in high school, I told my dad I wanted to learn how to cut hair and help people feel good about themselves. He said there was no way his daughter was going to be a barber; I was going to be a college graduate.

I'm glad that my father forced me to attend college. Those years are some of the most memorable of my life. But doing what *he* wanted me to do didn't get rid of my own desires. Years later, when I applied to barber school, I was afraid to tell my dad. I still felt a bit like I was betraying him.

Do you have people in your life whose opinions you put first? Think about the dreams and desires you've never pursued. People ask me all the time for psychic advice on what they're meant to be doing. We get so caught up in what we've been told we *should* be doing that we bury our dreams deep inside. We can lose sight of them for years on end.

Get out your journal and write about what you love to do. As the fellow at the AA meeting told me, look into your heart. Forget about the money it will take to make it happen.

Forget about not having the time. Forget about your age, and tune out the critical or authority figure voices in your head.

Think back to when you were a kid. What did you think you would be when you grew up? I once heard someone say that people usually know what they want to be when they are children. When I was a little girl, I would come home from school, line up all my dolls on my bed, and write everything on my chalkboard that I had learned that day. I couldn't wait to grow up and be a teacher. As it turns out, teaching psychic and healing classes has always been the most satisfying part of my work.

A dear friend of mine went back to college when he was sixty-seven. He was thrilled at the idea of getting his diploma by the time he turned seventy-one. "Now that my children are grown," he said, "and I don't have to scramble to support them, I can do what I want to do."

Another good friend decided at age forty-five to pursue her lifelong dream of being an attorney. She worked her way through night school. She didn't care that it was going to take a long time; she was just excited about finally following her dream.

Are you happy in your job, or would you rather be doing something else? If your answer is, "Something else," ask God for help overcoming the obstacles your mind sets up.

Find out what you need to do to reach your goal. Become willing to ask others for help. Take one step at a time — one baby step, if need be — but do take those steps. Be as persistent as I was with the barber school owner.

Our dreams are ours for a reason. Look where pursuing mine got me.

CHAPTER TEN

My New Career

IN FALL 1978, after relentless problems with my reproductive organs, I underwent a total hysterectomy. As a result of this surgery, I went through menopause at the age of twenty-nine. It was a very difficult time physically, mentally, and emotionally. It took about six months to regulate my hormone levels, but once that happened, life started to get back to normal — my "normal," that is.

My psychic abilities continued to grow stronger. Readings that used to last ten minutes now went for thirty. The healing energy that my body was channeling was becoming stronger as well.

Postsurgery, it was good to be back at work cutting hair. It was a great job, working with nice people, and the pay was very good. My growing abilities were a sign that another career change was coming, but I didn't want any more changes. My body had just been through so much. How would I know when it was really time to take another step on my professional path?

When I was in the hospital after being rear-ended by that drunk driver I told you about earlier, the doctors told me that I had suffered permanent damage to the nerves in my upper arms. They told me that as I got older, I would not have the full use of my arms. I was only twenty-four at the time of the accident. This future seemed so far away that I didn't take it all that seriously. My arms would heal on their own, I thought.

But in my fourth year of barbering, I started having pain in my upper arms after a long day of cutting hair. In my sobriety, there was no way I was getting back on pain pills. I received cortisone injections in my arms, neck, and back, but after a year of this, three doctors said it was time I found a new line of work.

I felt betrayed by God. Why was He letting this happen to me? Why did I have to leave a career I loved? Why hadn't He healed my arms?

I took a few weeks off and went to Florida to stay with a friend. During this break, I hoped to get guidance from God about what was next for me. Whenever my inner voice said, "You know what's next," I pretended not to hear. I *did* know it was time to start doing what I came here to do, but it made me feel so vulnerable. I liked the idea that I could control who knew about my abilities and when I would use my gifts. If I quit barbering and became a full-time healer and psychic, everyone would know this about me. It felt so exposing, and I hated that feeling. Was I strong enough to open myself up to all the people who distrusted, didn't believe, or just plain hated psychics?

I tried to look for the good, but it wasn't working very well. I was stuck in the groove of seeing only that I was being forced to quit something I loved in order to do something I was terrified of. It didn't seem fair. I knew from past experience that I should surrender to the plan, but surrender is rarely easy, and I hated it. Reluctantly, when I got back from Florida, I gave my month's notice at the barbershop.

The first seven months in my new career were just awful! I felt like the rich man in the Bible story, the one who wanted to be one of Jesus's disciples but couldn't when he learned he'd have to let go of all his material possessions. For me, it wasn't so much the material possessions I'd acquired during my good, steady job cutting hair; it was the mental shift that needed to take place within me. The focus of the work was different, and though I didn't mind living without some of the luxuries I'd had when I worked as a barber, it was a challenge to learn to measure my success in a different way. At the same time, I needed material concerns to take a backseat while I established myself in my new career, and this was tough. I felt I was doing what I was supposed to be doing, but I struggled to make ends meet.

While I worked at the shop, I had lots of nice clothes and a bunch of credit cards. I was able to pay my bills and taxes on time, had a new car, and lived in a nice place. Suddenly, I went from earning $500 a week (a great deal at the time) to $50 at best. I ate dinner at my mom's almost every night, and several times she made my car payments for me. I maxed out all my credit cards and even applied to General Assistance when my entire income for a month was $160. When GA told me I'd qualify for food stamps if I sold my car, I hit bottom. What was happening to me? If I was doing what God wanted me to do, why did I have to struggle so much?

My mom suggested that I ask God for a clear sign about what to do. Should I go back to barbering and put up with the pain in my arms, or was I really supposed to be doing psychic readings and healings for a living? I asked Him for a *very* clear sign so that I would stop wondering.

Within twenty-four hours of my request, a man for whom I had done a couple of readings called and asked if we could meet ASAP.

The next morning he said he had heard through the grapevine that I was doing readings full-time.

"How is it going?" he asked.

I told him the truth — that things were pretty tough — and that I wasn't sure whether to stick it out or go back to cutting hair. I also told him about my having asked God for a crystal-clear sign.

He proceeded to tell me that during his morning meditations that week, he was told to pay my rent for one year while I got on my feet. He asked God for guidance each day, he said, and for the last three mornings, he'd heard, "Pay Echo's rent for one year." He said he'd been worried about approaching me because he didn't want to insult me. *Insult me?* It took all the self-control I could muster not to jump up on the table and sing the Hallelujah Chorus. The only thing this man asked of me was that I keep our arrangement private.

With rent out of the way, I was able to make ends meet, even though business was still very slow. I did maybe one reading a day, and at $25, a reading didn't pay for much. I didn't know how to market myself, and it didn't feel right to put an ad in the paper. My inner guidance kept saying, "word of mouth," so I asked friends and relatives to spread the word.

After a few more months, and even with the help of my silent benefactor, I was again desperate and asked God for another sign. Once more, within twenty-four hours, I had my sign: a call from the local newspaper, the *Star and Tribune*. They were doing a story on several psychics in the Twin Cities area for Halloween and wanted to interview me.

The reporter and I spent an hour on the phone. She said that she and a photographer would come by the next day to take my photo. The photographer set up all kinds of lighting and began snapping pictures of me every time my facial expression changed. While this was going on, the reporter asked if I would give her a reading because her bosses wanted to see if I was any good. I was anxious about performing under this kind of pressure and didn't want anything to jeopardize the publicity I was about to get.

The reporter was pleased with the reading I gave, and still the photographer clicked away. I finally asked, "Why so many pictures?" That's when the reporter let me know that after our phone chat the day before, she and her editor had decided to make the story about me alone. She also said they'd nixed the Halloween angle.

On the day after Halloween, the story ran in the Variety section of the paper — with a picture of my face that covered a third of the page. Needless to say, my career took off like gangbusters. I had calls from all over the country and was suddenly booked a year in advance.

GOD DIMES

Barbering was not a detour from my path as a psychic and spiritual healer. Cutting hair taught me how to be self-employed, work with the public, set up appointments, and do bookkeeping. I learned how important it is to be disciplined and that no one else was going to do the work for me. If I wanted to succeed, I had to work hard.

One of the challenges of being self-employed is that you're never guaranteed a paycheck or a steady income. You can plan all you want, but so many variables can change things in a second — parents or children get sick and you have to take time off to care for them, or your own health prevents you from working. A slowdown in the economy can also slow you down, or a change in your field can force you to make a change. Here in Minnesota, even the weather plays a role. I never know how many students will show up to class each night, but when there's a threat of a tornado, ice storm, or blizzard, class — and a chunk of my income that month — is canceled.

An interesting thing started happening when I prayed for help with my finances: a dime would appear in a very strange place, followed closely by unexpected money that would always be enough to take care of my financial need. The first time this happened was when I prayed and then the article about me appeared, but it wasn't the last time. And when I say dimes in strange places, I mean strange — on top of the ketchup bottle in the refrigerator, in my shoe, in the bathtub, on my pillow, even on top of the steering wheel in my car. One day I was mowing the lawn, crying because I was thinking about an IRS debt I owed (more on that later). When I finished mowing, there was a perfect circle of dimes on my lawn!

I can be slow and stubborn when it comes to signs, but "God's dimes" were hard to miss, and even harder to misconstrue. I learned to trust that God had my back and that if I stayed on His path for me, the money I needed would — one way or another — meet me there.

CHAPTER ELEVEN

God in Stages

IN MY QUEST TO BETTER UNDERSTAND GOD — and prayer — three friends and I formed a prayer group called Master Mind. I'd heard about this kind of group at church. At our weekly meetings, we'd each share what we wanted help or guidance with, and one person would write down everyone's requests. At the next meeting, that person would read out loud the previous week's requests, and each of us would talk about how our prayers had been answered.

In our group, I learned about the power of prayer and the importance of being clear about what you're asking for. I saw that not all prayers are answered immediately. I learned about divine timing and that everything happens when it's meant to. No matter how much I pleaded for something, if it wasn't for my highest good, it wasn't going to happen.

I learned that if I prayed for things like patience, tolerance, and courage, life would present situations that required just those attributes. I remember once calling my mom and complaining, "Everyone's driving me crazy!" Mom asked what I had prayed for in my

Master Mind group, and when the word *patience* popped out of my mouth, we had a good laugh. God wasn't going to just hand me patience; He was going to show me that I already had it but wasn't using it.

In Master Mind, I also saw how my low self-esteem limited my sense of entitlement. For example, instead of praying for a brand-new car, I'd ask for one that works. Instead of asking for a hefty raise at work, I'd ask for enough money to get by.

By listening to what each group member prayed for, we all learned a great deal about each other and ourselves. We also became aware of the issues we had around trusting (mainly not trusting!) God.

When suffering with intestinal problems, I prayed to God for a healthy colon. After weeks of saying the same prayer, I landed in the hospital and needed emergency surgery. At first I felt let down that God hadn't healed me, but then it dawned on me that in order to *have* a healthy colon, I needed thirteen inches of "floppy intestines" removed. This was God's way of answering my prayer.

I wanted to be on a spiritual path more than I wanted any specific outcome I might pray for, so I started praying, "Thy will be done, not mine." I wanted any and all fear of God to go away so that we could be partners in life. I didn't want negative religious messages to interfere with God and I moving forward with each other. I wanted the trust that is essential to any good relationship. My Master Mind group showed me the areas that needed to heal so that I cold gain that trust. I realized that God wasn't a Santa Claus you could hand a list to.

We'd end each meeting with gratitude because we'd realized that ultimately, what we needed to do was surrender our will — our list — and instead ask for God to show us our highest good.

WHAT IS INTUITION?

You've probably noticed by now that I always turn to my intuition when making decisions or seeking guidance. Still, I didn't really understand this inner voice of mine until just a few years ago. My mother, who listened to her gut and taught me to pay attention to mine, simply called it "women's intuition."

My thirst to know God continued, and I began taking classes at the Unity Church, which I belonged to. One of the books we studied was *Lessons in Truth* by H. Emilie Cady. She refers to the "still, small voice within" as the voice of God. A lightbulb came on over my head. I asked my minister if Cady was saying that women's intuition was the voice of God. He confirmed that that was exactly what she was saying, except that we all have intuition, not just women. "Are you sure?" I asked him. My whole life I had expected to hear God as a booming voice from on high. It never occurred to me that the voice I had been listening to since I was a kid was actually God's soft, subtle knowingness. There's a passage in the Bible (Deuteronomy 18:15–18) that says that God's voice was so loud, people asked Him to please speak through the prophets. Could my inner knowing really be the voice of God?

Even though my minister was very clear about intuition being the voice of God, I wrestled with the idea until I read *Living in the Light* by Shakti Gawain. Gawain puts it a bit differently than Cady, saying that the inner knowing we all have in our gut is the voice of the Universe. Reading her words smacked me between the eyes. I finally got it.

Gawain writes that intuition never lies and is 100 percent accurate. It is not emotional. Feelings, our emotional responses, are not the same as intuition. I was like a Christmas tree, so many lightbulbs were coming on around me. I felt like someone had just given me the key to the Universe, and in a way, they had.

WHAT ABOUT MEDITATION?

As I read and asked questions about getting closer to God, the practice of meditation kept coming up. This was not an answer I wanted to hear, because it seemed impossible to quiet my mind. People were also talking about God being within us, and this went right over my head. I had been raised to believe that God was in heaven, far, far away above the clouds.

I sat in a lotus position. I closed my eyes. I did the "om" thing. Nothing happened, other than my mind wandering to my grocery or chore list. I felt like a failure at meditation, so I minimized its value.

One day I got the inner nudge to call my friend Roy, who meditated daily. Could he explain the concept of Higher Self and teach me to meditate? Roy said that the Higher Self is the part of us that is God and that we meditate to communicate with this presence.

My mind jumped back to a class I'd attended at Unity. There I'd heard that there was a personal God and an impersonal God. The personal God resided inside us, while the impersonal God resided outside us and watched over the world. My mind grappled with these new ideas, and later that night, I asked God to help me understand them.

Meanwhile, I kept trying — and failing — to meditate. Then one day I had a breakthrough. I was running on a treadmill and for some reason grabbed onto the bars, closed my eyes, put my attention on my belly button, and asked God, "Are you in there?"

Suddenly, a white light came out of my midsection, and I heard a male voice say, "Yes, I am." My first impulse was to jump off the machine and run! But I stayed and watched the light emanating from my solar plexus. I felt peaceful. The more I concentrated on it, the more peaceful I got. After a while, I wanted to stay on that treadmill forever. I stayed with this unusual experience until the light disappeared.

The next day, when I got back on the treadmill and again asked God if He was within me, a beautiful white energy came out of my solar plexus. It took the form of a sword, like Excalibur, and I had the sense of this light being my protector.

I believe I was able to experience this because on the treadmill, my mind was busy keeping my feet on the track. Because I wasn't desperately trying to quiet my mind, I was freed up to hear the voice. As the communications became lengthier, I began to keep a notebook by the treadmill so that I wouldn't forget all the information I was receiving — insight into the gift of healing and my psychic abilities, guidance about clients, advice on my personal journey.

I finally understood why meditation is so important. Studying about meditation, in classes and books and at church, had only given me head knowledge. Now I *knew*, quite literally, in my gut. I was in touch with my Higher Self and getting to know God. It was wonderful. My thirst was finally being quenched.

After several years of talking to Him, the feeling of this powerful male presence within me changed and became softer, more feminine. I felt a shift in who I was talking to. I asked the female voice what had happened to God, and She said that She was the feminine side of God. She would now be working with me for a while. "Could I ask the real God if this is okay?" I asked Her. She had a good chuckle at that.

The Bible verse telling us that we are made in God's image and likeness (Genesis 1:26) came into my head. I realized that if that was true, there *must* be a female side to God. We aren't all men, after all. I had to ponder this because I had been raised to believe God was male. Once again, old teachings were being booted out. I had asked to know the real God, and I was being shown the real God.

It took time for me to adjust to the female half of my Higher

Self, but once I accepted Her wholeheartedly, the male side began talking to me again. I now hear both. And meditation is no longer restricted to treadmill time. I spend the majority of my day in silence, receiving guidance from both the male and female sides of my Higher Self. This is the most peaceful and beautiful way I have ever lived.

FOR YOU TO THINK ABOUT

Your Meditation Practice

Do you meditate? If so, write in your journal how your practice got started for you and how it has changed over time.

If you do not meditate, write down what might be keeping (or blocking) you from doing so. Also write down what you feel you would need in order to meditate.

Do you know that prayer is talking to God, and meditation is God talking back? We need to give our inner voice time each day to express itself.

I want you to try sitting in silence for at least five minutes every other day. Just sit, close your eyes, and ask God if He/She has any messages for you. Keep your focus on your solar plexus area (just below the rib cage). When you find that you have more time, do this for longer periods.

If your day is absolutely packed with activities from morning till night, then I want you to write down when, during that hectic schedule of yours, you are all by yourself. In the bathroom? In traffic? At lunchtime? During a coffee break? I guarantee that when you're ready to give God some time to talk back, you will find the time — and be grateful that you did.

PART TWO

Living and Growing Spiritually

I WAS FIFTEEN WHEN I FIRST READ *Sermon on the Mount* by Emmet Fox, and I remember being so struck by the teachings of Jesus. I wanted desperately to go out and teach what He taught because I knew intuitively that if people heard His teachings, they would find peace inside.

I also thought that there was no way I could learn to be spiritual while living in the city. I figured the only way I would be able to know all the great things the master teachers knew was by living on a mountaintop, with all the gurus who lived there. My sweet, naive, fifteen-year-old mind thought that the only way to bring wisdom to people was by learning it from the great master teachers first.

I told God that there was just too much other stuff to think about living in the suburbs; if I was on top of some mountain, I could absorb spiritual teachings so much better. I was extremely disappointed when I heard a male voice tell me that I needed to learn how to find inner peace, and live the principles in Jesus's Sermon on the Mount right where I was.

Like any teenager, I didn't want to have to wait until I got older. I didn't want it to take years for me to become a wise person. I wanted to be a spiritual teacher *now*.

Slowly, over time, I realized that life itself was teaching me to be a spiritual teacher. Donning a candy striper's uniform (tried that) hadn't given me instant wisdom. Becoming a missionary (looked into that) wasn't necessarily going to make me a spiritual person. Living on top of a mountain (is that where gurus really live?) wouldn't address the problems of the people I wanted to help. I had to learn wisdom and grow spiritually *through* life experiences. My lessons came firsthand and were learned over and over and sometimes over again.

Being on this path has been a blessing in so many ways. I've had experiences I could never have imagined having — and probably wouldn't have had on some mountaintop. I know it's all because I've grown up to have a childlike faith that God is watching over me and wants me to do well.

My deep, internal desire to serve God and people has kept me going through the rough times. I admit there have been times when I truly wanted to hang it all up and get a "regular" job. I've wondered where people get the idea that it's okay to be rude, critical, and insensitive toward people with psychic abilities. Fundamentalists, skeptics, cynics, and just all-around nasty people have it in their heads that these gifts are false or even satanic.

But when I look back over my career, the negative experiences pale in comparison to how amazing the good ones have been. I've seen countless miracles in my healing work, and because I've lived by the still, small voice within, I always end up at the right place at the right time. Who brings these cool experiences into my life? They are totally divine in nature.

In the next chapters, I'd like to share some additional stories from my life, in no particular order. It's through these experiences that I learned to differentiate spirituality from religion. I believe that these events have given me insight into what's going on behind the scenes in life — and that they'll do the same for you.

CHAPTER TWELVE

Right Place, Right Time

I WAS ON A BOOK TOUR FOR MY THIRD BOOK, *Echoes of the Soul*, and had some time to spare while out on the West Coast. I decided to visit a girlfriend who had just moved to Malibu. It was absolutely beautiful there. My friend lived right on the beach, so three times a day, I would walk up and down it, watching the ocean and looking at the amazing homes. On one of my walks, I talked out loud to God about how much I loved it there and how I wished there was a way for me to come back often.

The next morning, I had breakfast with my friend and her personal trainer. He casually mentioned that he'd never had a psychic reading and would love one. I asked him if there were specific things he wanted to know about, and when he said, "Marriage," I opened up psychically. I gave him a lot of personal information that he called "amazing." He then asked if I'd be open to giving readings to three of his friends. These friends just happened to own the Malibu Health Club and, to make a long story short, after I gave each of them a reading, they asked if I would like to work at their club.

They would do all the advertising and scheduling of appointments; all I needed to do was let them know when I would be in town.

For two years (until my practice in Minnesota became too busy), I went back and forth between Minnesota and Malibu. I loved Malibu, the scenery, the ocean, the people. It was a great time in my life — and it started with a simple prayer.

During another visit to California, I had dinner with a producer friend. Her production company was winding up their taping of a reality show about Farrah Fawcett. My friend asked if I'd like to stop by Farrah's while she dropped off some things for her crew. The thought of meeting Farrah Fawcett was so cool, of course I wanted to tag along.

When Farrah came into the living room, my hands immediately heated up. She was talking about feeling low in energy, so I asked if she'd like me to channel some healing to her.

Another producer in the room asked if I would mind if they taped this. I sat next to Farrah on the couch and simply put my hand on her leg. She could feel the heat and said she loved it. Someone mentioned that I was a ghostbuster (more on this in a later chapter), so Farrah asked if her place was haunted. I could feel that there were no spirits in the house, but she said she'd feel better if I did a walk-through. With camera crew in tow, I checked the place out and found nothing. I returned to the couch, continued to channel healing energy to Farrah, and did a short reading for her. When we were done, Farrah was flying high with energy and thanked me effusively for coming to her home.

A few weeks later, when the reality show aired, I was on-screen for much of the fun episode. It was all very exciting for me — especially because they were respectful of me and my abilities.

But there's more: I had been concerned about my finances

before making this trip out West. When I boarded my flight to return home, I found a dime on the floor in front of my seat. I looked up, smiled, and wondered what God had up Her sleeve. Sure enough, two days later I received a check from the production company, thanking me for the work I had done with Farrah.

Another of my many experiences of right place, right time also involves a celebrity. I was twenty-one and working at Uncle John's Pancake House as the night manager. We were open until 2:00 AM, to serve the bar crowd, and on this night, I neglected to lock the front door after the last customer had left. I was in the back counting out the money; Duane, the cook, had just finished cleaning the grill; and Madelyn, the waitress, was just about done setting the tables for the morning shift. I heard someone walk in the front door yelling, "Hello, are you open? Can we get some food?"

I ran out front, and there stood comedian Bob Hope with his wife and two friends. I looked at Duane, and he gave me a "don't you dare make me dirty my grill" look. I knew Madelyn was beat and anxious to get home. I politely told Hope and company that we were closed but that they might try the open-all-night restaurant up the road, Embers.

After a few minutes, when Duane, Madelyn, and I had had a moment to think, we all jumped in my car. We had to go to Embers to see if it was really Bob Hope we'd just been with. As we drove up the road, there, above the Embers restaurant in Edina, Minnesota, we saw a flying saucer hovering over the building! I slammed on my brakes, and we all got out to stare up at the sky.

"It" just sat there, swaying back and forth. It was gray and shaped like a saucer. We looked at it and at each other in speechless wonder.

A few moments later, an orange light shot out of the bottom of the saucer, it moved up just a bit, and then it disappeared. At that point, we were all so freaked out that we no longer cared about seeing Bob Hope, and we turned around and went home.

Thirty years later, I was driving my ten-year-old niece to a birthday party. She was showing signs of having psychic abilities and asked if I had ever seen a UFO. The two of us were on the same road and in the exact same spot where Duane, Madelyn, and I had, in fact, seen the flying saucer. "Why do you ask?" I said to my niece. She replied that the image of a UFO had just popped into her head.

CHAPTER THIRTEEN

Reincarnation

BACK IN 1966, when my psychic teacher, Birdie Torgeson, taught our psychic development class about reincarnation, I didn't want anything to do with it. I didn't want to hear that I had lived before or that I might be coming back again. Life was hard enough without having to worry about what I did in past lives and what karmic debts I might have racked up as a result.

I remember thinking that since I was young, I could put the issue of reincarnation on a back burner. Instead, as my psychic abilities developed, I began getting images of past lives while doing readings. I wanted to rationalize the information away. Couldn't these images be symbols, or just my imagination running wild?

One day a woman I was reading asked if I could help her understand her relationship with her significant other. The first image that came to me was of a male doctor in the 1800s. I then saw my client in a nurse's uniform and knew that she was this doctor's assistant. I could see that the man was alcoholic, that she continually covered for him, and that she resented him terribly for this. The doctor eventually drank himself to death. My client's soul still wanted recognition from him for all that she had done in that life. The doctor and nurse were very dependent on each other and needed to break that pattern. In order to move on, she needed to forgive him.

My client told me that these scenes perfectly described her current relationship. She'd even attended nursing school in this life.

This woman didn't know if she believed in reincarnation any more than I did. But she felt that the information I provided helped her understand her current situation.

As more past-life information came through in my readings, I knew I had to let go of my resistance to it. With half an open mind, I went back to my teacher and asked her to explain reincarnation to me again. Hearing her explanation of past lives and karma had a very positive impact on my relationship with God. If all the things that were happening in my life were happening so that my soul had opportunities to grow, then there was no one to blame. If all the bad stuff in my life wasn't happening because God was punishing me (that old religious training), then none of it was God's "fault." This meant I really could turn to Him when I needed Him. I didn't have to be afraid of Him (which is how I thought of God at the time) any longer. This was a dramatic and liberating shift in my understanding.

I didn't love the idea of karma — paying off old debts — simply because I didn't know what my soul had been up to in its past lives! But intellectually, it all made sense. Still, I had a kernel of doubt until another experience convinced me that reincarnation is real.

It was back in 1974. My mom attended a spiritualist convention and met a nice young man, whom I will call Roy. They became fast friends, and Mom was anxious for me to meet him. He and I were the same age, and he was as interested in spiritual healing as I was. Mom tried several times to arrange our meeting, but something always got in the way. On my end, this was partially because I had an inner nervousness about him that I didn't understand.

One evening, Mom invited me over for dinner without telling

me she'd also invited Roy. When he walked into the house, I turned to shake his hand, and my soul began to react. I felt all kinds of emotions racing inside, and I wanted to bolt.

Within minutes of Roy's arrival, I began to see images. Every time I looked at him or heard his voice, I saw scenes of a farmhouse in Germany. A brown farmhouse. Children running all around. A man and a woman farming the fields.

I could not control or stop these images. Then I heard myself say to Roy, "Do you remember that we were married in a past life, in Germany?" I put my hand over my mouth, but the words kept coming. "We were farmers. We had many children." I didn't say, "Nine children," though that's what I saw.

Roy became agitated. He didn't know what I was talking about and said he didn't believe in reincarnation. I apologized and tried pulling myself together, but it was as if something was going on that I had no control over.

We all sat down to dinner, and Roy mentioned that he was sorry his wife hadn't been able to join us. Again, I spoke without wanting or meaning to. "I'm your wife! Wait, I'm sorry. I know I'm not your wife." I felt so out of control that I got up from the table and went and stood in the hall closet — the only place I could think to hide in. I was absolutely, inappropriately, and uncontrollably enraged at the thought of Roy being with another woman. I could barely tolerate the way I felt.

My mom came into the closet and asked what on earth was going on. I told her I had no idea because I had never had these kinds of feelings before. Where were they coming from? I had never experienced such deep feelings of jealousy in this lifetime. I wanted Mom to explain it all to me, but she was just as baffled as I was.

Once again, I composed myself and went back to the table. I apologized to Roy, explaining that the pictures in my head and the feelings I was having felt very real.

Quite innocently, Roy mentioned his wife again, and I lashed out as before. "I'm your wife. Don't you remember? We've made love more than a thousand times." I could actually feel the sensation in my body of being with him intimately. I could see our bedroom and the house full of children. I was a big woman, and he was a big man. When my eyes were closed, I saw everything, plain as day.

Understandably, Roy didn't linger after dinner, and I was very relieved when he left. He called the next day to see if I was feeling better, and just hearing his voice took me right back into all the feelings. We decided it was best to stay away from each other for the time being.

Several months later, Roy called to ask if he could bring his cousin to me for a healing. He expressed interest in observing and perhaps working with me. He arrived a few days later with a beautiful blonde — and the vibe between them was definitely not cousin-like. I felt rage start to rise within me but managed to be civil to the poor girl.

When Roy ran out to his car to get a book for me, I went into the kitchen to get this woman a cup of coffee. I commented on her being Roy's cousin, and she told me that his cousin had to cancel at the last minute and that she and Roy were dating. She also told me that Roy and his wife had split up. That deep rage started again, and the only thing I could think to do was go into the hall closet again. When Roy came back, she told him where I was.

Roy came looking for me, and I asked him to please get her out of there. I told him I felt this deep hatred that I just couldn't explain, and I didn't want to hurt her (I was having thoughts of throwing hot coffee on her).

The next day, when Roy called to see how I was doing, we once again agreed not to talk to each other until I could get this all sorted out. I hated the way I felt when I was around him. It just wasn't the me I recognized.

Several months later, Roy called to tell me that he'd been to see a past-life regressionist. He'd been able to see several of his past lives, including ours in Germany. "Brown farmhouse, right? Nine children? You were a big woman."

He said he saw very clear pictures explaining why I was so jealous. In this past life, each Saturday night he went into town to drink and be with a prostitute. The next morning, when I went into town to attend church, the women from church would tell me what my husband had done the night before. Because I was such a stoic woman, I kept all my feelings inside. I probably didn't know how to talk about the rage I felt back then. But here I was, lifetimes later, finally getting the feelings out.

Roy told me that he now knew he came into this lifetime to make amends with me. Part of our karma this lifetime was to learn how to communicate with each other and possibly work together as healers.

We began speaking on the phone regularly and developed a special friendship. I found that if I kept my eyes open when we talked, I could stay in the present.

We've remained close friends and always feel a bond when we're around each other. What's more, when any of our nine children from this past life come into my current life, I recognize them. Though Roy and I move in separate circles, we've found that our "children" invariably know Roy as well.

FOR YOU TO THINK ABOUT

People You May Have "Known" Before

My psychic teacher told me that anyone who is more than an acquaintance in our lives is someone from a past life.

Are there people in your life to whom you feel a special or strange connection? A kind of kinship you can't explain, a feeling of familiarity, or even an inexplicable dislike or antagonism?

Are there times in history that you are drawn to or times that you have an aversion to and just don't want to hear about? Every year in the fall, a Renaissance Festival comes to Minnesota. The one and only time I ever went to it was with Roy, and I felt physically sick and claustrophobic when we were there and couldn't wait to leave. I've never gone back.

Do you have unexplained fears or phobias? If they are not based on something that happened to you in this life, you can bet you brought them in from a former life. A lot of experiences from past lives carry over and continue to affect us until we let go of the emotions of the experience. In readings, I've seen that souls will carry unresolved emotions for lifetimes rather than trying to heal them.

If any relationships in your life are troublesome or feel strange, write about them in your journal. By getting the details down on paper, you may become aware of past-life connections. This could help you, as it did Roy, to see what you came here to do together in this lifetime. If you have a particularly difficult relationship, you might consider going to a past-life regressionist to shed some light on it.

If you aren't sure what you believe about reincarnation, there are excellent books to help you get a better understanding of it. My book *Echoes of the Soul* has fascinating stories in it, and I'd suggest starting there.

CHAPTER FOURTEEN

Journey to the Other Side

IT WAS THE BEGINNING OF SPRING 1992. The sun was shining, birds were singing, the earth was coming alive again after a long winter in Minnesota. It was Palm Sunday, and I was torn between going to church and doing what I wanted to do — preparing my garden for planting. I felt like I *should* be in church, but I wanted to be in the quiet of my yard and to talk to God there. I followed the guidance of my inner voice and spent the morning outside.

My brother Michael is a very gifted psychic who has been seeing spirits/ghosts since he was a little boy. Twenty years earlier, I got a call from a woman who thought her house was haunted. I asked my brother if he would come with me, since I was a bit of a chicken. That night, without even meaning to, we started a career as a ghostbusting team.

Michael and I had been on a ghostbusting job the previous night, and I went to bed thinking about the other side. When I woke up that Palm Sunday morning, it was still on my mind. As I was working in my garden, I was thinking of the knowledge about heaven I had gained over the years. I had learned quite a bit from readings I had channeled and had gathered bits and pieces while communicating with the deceased. Still, I had no real, experiential knowledge. I had been ghostbusting for twenty years, always believing that I was sending those souls to a good place. That day, both for myself and for my clients, I wanted more concrete information.

As I worked in the garden, I asked God if I could please learn more about the other side. Three days later, after completely forgetting my prayer, I had the most memorable experience of my career.

It was Wednesday; I had just finished a healing session with Neil, a good friend, and he was heading upstairs from my basement office. My office started to fill with a hazy white energy. I felt strange, weak, as if I was going to collapse. In my body it felt like I had fallen asleep, yet I was awake. I didn't recognize it as such at the time, but I was beginning to have an out-of-body experience.

I became aware of a woman, in spirit form, standing in front of me. I couldn't see her face, just the back of her head and her long blonde hair. She said to me, "Let's go, let's go." I felt afraid and asked Neil to help me. I told him something very strange was happening and that a presence was urging me to follow her.

My perceptions were completely off. I knew on one level that I was in my office, but I also felt as if I were in another dimension. Neil shook my body, hoping to stop whatever was happening. It did stop for a few seconds but then started up again, with the spirit urging me to go with her. I told Neil that I felt like I was dying.

Meanwhile, the room continued to fill with white fog, and my body became so weak that I wanted just to lie down and let go.

Then I became aware of a tunnel directly in front of me. It was the same tunnel I had seen in so many of my ghostbusting jobs, the tunnel I sent ghosts through and into the light, the tunnel that connects our side to the other side.

One of my spirit guides directed me to have Neil contact Michael and ask him to come over, and then get me upstairs and into the living room. By this point I could barely speak, and my legs were lifeless. Neil kept telling me to get back into my body, and the blonde spirit kept telling me to go with her. Neil dragged me to the couch, and my body fell into a heap.

Minutes seemed like hours as we waited for my brother to arrive. When Michael finally came, he understood what was happening. He had talked with his guides on the drive over, and they told him that three days earlier I had asked God for a better understanding of the other side. They told him I was being allowed to actually go over and that I would consciously remember the experience.

My brother told me, "Echo, I am supposed to hold your hand and ground your body while your soul goes to the other side and gathers information." As he was talking, I realized that the blonde spirit was my soul, trying to get me to let go and move on to the other side.

Michael took my hand and told me that everything was fine, that I should go, and that he would be here to protect my body. With his reassurance, my soul completely left my body, and my conscious mind was with me. I started to float through the tunnel. A loving warmth surrounded me. Throughout the tunnel, I heard a faint voice echoing, "Let go, let go."

Many souls were in the tunnel waiting to greet departing (dying) loved ones. Reunions were taking place around me. Then I saw a bright light ahead, at the end of the tunnel. I floated up, going higher and higher. As I came up to the white light, I remember thinking that I should close my eyes or I would be blinded by its brightness — but I opened my eyes instead and flowed right through the light.

I came out on the other side feeling calm and aware. I could see a quaint little village with cobblestoned streets. My grandmother was standing there with a friend. She introduced me, and her friend said, "Oh, you didn't tell me she was dying today." My grandmother replied, "Oh, no, she's not dying, just visiting." I looked closely at my grandma's face. She looked so beautiful — no wrinkles, no stress, just joy. Youthfulness and serenity engulfed her. I looked around and saw several old friends who had died. They didn't come over to me; they just smiled as if they knew I was not to waste any time. They all had that same youthful, serene look on their faces.

Out of nowhere, an angel appeared. She was quite lovely, with wavy, light-reddish hair down to her shoulders, a long flowing gown, and, yes, wings. She told me she would be my guide and wanted to show me as much as possible in the limited time we had.

The first place she took me was called the Pink Place. The entire community had a pink aura around it. It was beautiful. In front of us was a hospital, and even though we were standing some distance from it, I could see inside. It wasn't like a hospital on earth, with a lot of medical equipment and personnel. It was more like a resting place, with caregivers. They were not necessarily doctors or nurses, simply helpers.

Some souls in the hospital were going through an adjustment period, learning to live without their physical bodies. Many had been heavily medicated during their death process, and their souls were affected by the drugs. They were resting, healing, and adjusting. Some souls had difficulty accepting their deaths; caregivers worked with them to help them with their transition. Some souls from physically handicapped bodies needed to adjust to life without challenged bodies. A large section of the hospital was for suicide victims. Some were asleep; others were dealing with their frustration over having taken their own lives. Many were still knocked out from the amount of drugs or alcohol they had taken to bring on their deaths.

Next, we floated down a road. I first saw a landscape with rolling hills, lush foliage, grass, flowers, streams, lakes, and rivers. The flowers were fragrant, and their colors were crisp and vivid. We continued floating over a hill and into a valley, where I saw a huge white-and-gold coliseum with enormous pillars, windows, and doors, but no glass. I saw angels coming in and out. I was told that this was where the angels who help people on earth live.

At about this time, I heard my brother prompting me, "Go find the music." I then became aware that music was playing all around me. The angel and I floated to a meadow filled with singers and musicians. I saw — of all people! — Nat King Cole, and then many others whom I recognized from this side. Some were writing songs; some were singing. This is a little hard to describe, but several kinds of music were being played at the same time. It was like a giant radio station; you could "tune in" to what you wanted to hear.

The next city we floated to was particularly important to me. As I've written, Jesus has been a central figure to me for as long as I can remember. Now we were in a magnificent place, truly a place of beauty — blue sky, lush green nature everywhere. Thousands of souls were milling around, very excited about something. It felt as if a celebration were going on. People were very emotional; some were cheering, others crying. Still others stood off by themselves, completely captivated by the man in the middle of the crowd. He was speaking or teaching about something. I looked at the angel as if to ask her who the man was. "Jesus," she said.

I wondered if it was okay for me to be there. The angel, reading my thoughts, told me it was fine. I was welcome. She had wanted me to experience the City of Jesus (as she called it), knowing what He meant to me.

I felt great joy and awe as I watched Him preach. Here was the man I cherished so much. He was surrounded by a golden aura that radiated wisdom and knowledge. His features were striking — dark shoulder-length hair, a beard, a dark complexion, and the most intense eyes I had ever seen. Yet the thing I found myself mesmerized by were His hands: strong, weathered, thousands of years old, full of wisdom and knowledge from all the pain He had healed.

He talked to an enormous crowd of souls about loving one another. His whole message, His whole essence, was love. There was such a gentleness about Him. He felt so powerful, and yet He was humble. I wanted to get as close to Him as possible. I remember feeling as if I were truly *home*. I didn't want to leave. Everywhere I looked the air seemed charged with hope, with answers.

I could hear my brother's voice telling me my body was having a difficult time. "Hurry up," he said. He told me to look for God, and I realized that I was surrounded by God. God was and is everywhere. Just think the word *God*, and God is there. A presence. A knowingness.

Again Michael urged me to come back. I asked the angel what else she could teach me before I returned to my body.

She told me that heaven was full of communities and that each reflected a different reality. The reality we live by on earth, the consciousness we hold, determines where we go in heaven. For example, if during your lifetime you were a hard-working, devout Catholic, when you go to heaven, you will live in a community that embraces the same beliefs. She showed me a community of beggars and thieves. She said that is their reality. All day long, they steal or beg from one another. Eventually they will grow tired of that way of life and start asking souls outside their community if there is a better way to live. All souls continually move on to different realities, always searching for a better way. People need to evolve in their beliefs while in heaven, just as they must on earth. Each soul needs to learn and grow toward its oneness with God.

I said that it seemed complicated to have so many communities with varying realities. She replied that it is actually less complicated than it is on earth, for in heaven everyone is clear about each other's realities. If you live in a community different from others', you have a different belief system than they do. It's that simple. She said that it's more complex on earth because we believe that we all have the same reality when, in fact, we don't. She said that we have so many problems on earth because we have trouble honoring each other's convictions. We don't want to accept that everyone has a different reality; we want everyone to be and think and act as we do.

Because I'm such a movie buff, I asked the angel about movie stars. She said that they also have their own community and may live there if they choose to remain stars. Some who cross over desire a change from their movie star identity and go to a community that better reflects their individuality and reality.

The comedian Sam Kinison had died about two weeks before I had this "tour." I'm a Kinison fan and was curious to know how he was doing. I asked the angel about him, and she motioned me to an area where I saw him standing on a road. I could hear his laughter. There were many souls around him, shaking his hand, congratulating him on doing such a good job while on earth. I looked at the angel, somewhat baffled by what they were saying. To my mind, Sam was a bit crude in his performances; it surprised me to hear people saying, "Good job!" The angel smiled and told me that he had indeed accomplished what he came to earth to do. His job had been to get people to think about their beliefs, their values, their morals, and he'd accomplished this.

As I watched Kinison in his big overcoat, beret, and tennis shoes, shaking hands and laughing with people, I heard my brother again, sternly calling me back. I could tell by the tone of his voice that I had to go. To my right I saw a broad stairway, and I asked the angel where it led. She said that there are several levels to heaven. The highest level is where we all have the same reality, where we know we are one with God and live in peace with one another.

I asked the angel one last question. Was the village with the cobblestoned streets, where I had arrived, the entrance point to heaven? She said it was one of many places throughout heaven where people arrived. Some went directly to the hospital; others went to entry points determined by their consciousnesses. She said that she wished she could teach me and show me so much more, but my body was really suffering and I had to go back. As soon as she spoke those words, my soul jolted back into my body.

When I took this conscious journey out of my body, I used all the energy in my soul to do it. My body experienced a great deal of difficulty while I was out. I was like a rag doll, lifeless and limp. After my soul came back in, it took at least twenty minutes before I could speak. My tongue was thick, and my eyes had trouble opening and were very sensitive to light. It took a great effort to move my body for some time. At least an hour passed before I felt normal again. As soon as I was able to go to bed, I slept for twelve hours.

The days that followed were somewhat difficult. I didn't want to be here anymore. I wished I could be on the other side; it felt like home, and I missed it. I could now understand the ambivalence I have seen in souls who are preparing to reincarnate because they are looking at it as work, almost like going back to school. The other side is where we get to relax and take a break, so it's no wonder I've seen many souls drag their feet about coming back here.

CHAPTER FIFTEEN

Pictures of the Soul

IN FALL 1986, a client called and asked if I would look at some
pictures taken at the scene of a car accident. She said there was a
strange energy in them and wondered if it was the soul of the person killed in the incident. She went on to explain that when the police
officer at the scene took the pictures, he saw nothing unusual in the
viewfinder. When they were developed, he was quite surprised at
what appeared.

The accident in the photos involved four teenagers on their way
to a rock concert. It was winter in Minnesota, the roads were icy, and
their car hit a patch of ice and skidded off the road. The passenger
in the front seat hit the dash and fatally broke his neck.

The first picture I saw was of this teen laying peacefully on the
front seat of the car. It wasn't gruesome, but there was white light
coming out of his mouth in the shape of a hook. There was other
energy in the picture as well, but not as strong as the energy coming out of his body. The policeman took the second photo from the
backseat, and you could see more of this streaming energy coming

out of the middle of the young man's back. The third picture was filled with what looked like streamers of energy. Energy was all over the picture; nothing else was visible. And the fourth photo, well, that one blew all of us away. The cop had stepped back and taken an overall shot of the car. In this photo, a head was visible above the car, a head that appeared to be screaming. It looked angry and as if it were saying, "Nooooooo!" I looked back at the first picture and realized that the screaming head was clearly that of the teen who'd hit the dash.

At this time, I had a spirit guide named John who helped me in my psychic work. I asked him to help me interpret the pictures. He said that the streams of energy were the boy's soul slowly exiting his body. He said that the soul was confused about what was happening and that's why it came out in streams rather than all at once. John said the boy's soul started to come together in its whole form in the fourth photograph. The cop just happened to snap the shot at the very moment the head had formed.

I asked John why the boy looked so angry. "He's sixteen, on his way to a rock concert with his buddies, and suddenly his physical body is dead," he said. I stared at those pictures for the longest time, trying to comprehend what I was seeing.

I asked my client if I could have a copy of the pictures to show my students. She said there was no way the policeman would let me have them. The family of the deceased hadn't seen the pictures, and the officer was ambivalent about showing them to people. I pleaded with her to convince him that I would not misuse the pictures in any way. "Don't count on it," she told me.

A few months went by, and I could not stop thinking about the pictures. I called my client and asked her to set up a meeting for me with the policeman. I wanted him to see that I was a person of integrity and that I would not do anything disrespectful — like sell the pictures to the *National Enquirer*. She called a few days later to say that he was willing to meet with me, but that he was *not* going to release the pictures. He also stipulated that he did not want me to know his name or where he worked.

From the way my client had spoken of this cop, I expected a crabby old guy to show up at the restaurant that night. He turned out to be quite the opposite. As soon as he walked into the restaurant I *recognized* him on a soul level; it was as if I had previously known him. The officer was in his early forties, quite handsome, and very charming. His presence was commanding and even intimidating. I wanted to impress him with my sincerity, but he made me nervous.

At the time of our meeting I had just started working on my book *Echoes of the Soul*, which is about the soul's perspective of life, death, and life after death. I wanted the officer's permission to put his amazing pictures in the book. He said he would talk to his captain. If the captain said it was okay to release the pictures to me, he would. He also asked that all our communication take place through the client who initially brought me the photos. I anxiously waited for her to call with my answer. Unfortunately, a week later I got a "no go."

I was very frustrated. An actual photo of a soul existed, and I could not get my hands on it. I asked God, "Why, why, why was I given a glimpse of these remarkable photos but no access to them?" Since I'd been called about them, it felt like I was *meant* to do something with them. I asked God to please pull whatever strings He could to get me those photographs.

A year passed, and I again thought of the pictures. I called the go-between and asked her to set up another meeting for me with the policeman. He agreed to meet with the two of us, at my client's house. While we were looking at the photos again, he and I noticed something for the first time: the image of a dog, sitting by the front door of the car. Even more surprising, my client recognized the dog. She said it had belonged to the dead boy. The dog, she went on, had died about a year *before* the car accident.

Once again, I did my best to reassure the cop that I was not going to exploit the pictures. Could I please, please have copies? He had a new captain and said he would check with him. The officer was trying to get a promotion and didn't want anything to interfere. He'd ask, he said, when the timing felt right.

It was months before I heard anything, and when I did, the answer was not only, "No," but also, "Please leave me alone." My inner voice told me to be patient and not to give up. I could still write about the pictures in my book, which I did.

When I turned in my manuscript, the publisher called and said he wanted to include the photos in the book. I laughed and told him it would be easier for me to break into Fort Knox. "Do what you gotta do," he insisted. "Get me those photographs."

I hung up the phone, looked up at the heavens, and told God I needed His help. Remember, I didn't know the policeman's name or where he worked. God clearly had His work cut out for him — and I'd need to do some detective work myself.

Shortly after my prayer, something the officer said to me during our first meeting popped into my head. I called information and got the number of a precinct I had a hunch about. When I dialed and asked for "the officer in vice who wears dark-rimmed glasses," the man on the other end of the line laughed. "I need more information than that, ma'am." I stammered a bit. "Well, there's this policeman . . . who took some pictures. . . ." The man then blurted out, "Oh, are you the psychic over in Minneapolis?" Rather surprised, I said that yes, I was. He then put me through to the cop's voice mail.

Now I knew the officer's name and where he worked. But he'd told me to leave him alone. I prayed for courage as the officer's line rang. When his voice mail came on, I took a deep breath and in one very fast sentence, left a cheerful message about being someone from his past who wasn't going away. Could we please meet again? I'd finished my book, I explained, and my publisher was insisting that I get those pictures. I left my number, exhaled, and waited all weekend for his call.

Early Monday morning I got a very nice message. He'd be happy to meet — but I shouldn't expect the photos.

A few days later, we met for lunch at a restaurant and caught up. He'd gotten his promotion and was doing well. When the conversation turned to the pictures, he looked at me and said, "Bodine, I don't know what it is about you, but I trust you." Then he reached into his briefcase and handed me the negatives. He said that enough time had now passed, and since the family had no interest in seeing the photographs, he was comfortable giving me a copy of them. He said that I should take the negatives to photo specialists and get documented letters from experts confirming that the photos were not doctored and that they had been made from the original negatives.

He said I could have the negatives for two weeks and make as many copies as I wanted, but then he wanted them back. I thought he was being a little paranoid about people not believing the pictures were real, but I soon found out that not everyone was as excited about them as I was.

One specialist said that the camera's shutter must have gotten stuck because of the cold; that's why there was all this "stuff" in them. Another flat-out refused to deal with the images — and walked away from me. Yet another said there was no way to be certain I hadn't stuck a boy's face in a picture, taken a photo of *that* picture, and then made the negatives. All of them agreed the pictures were very old. Yes, the photos were unusual, but no one would confirm anything "on the record."

When I showed the photos to my students, I got even more theories. Maybe it was the ambulance driver's face superimposed above the car, and so on.

Then there was my publisher. I very excitedly overnighted the photos to him, and he was as unconvinced as the others. He felt they had been somehow doctored, and therefore he wouldn't put them in my book. If they were real, he said, they were just too "scary."

If you'd like to decide for yourself about these images, you can see them on my website, www.echobodine.com.

By the way, over the years the police officer and I have become good friends. We swap emails from time to time, just to check in. I believe that before we came into this lifetime, our souls made an agreement about these photos: he would take them, and I would get them out in the world — with God's help and in God's time, not in mine.

CHAPTER SIXTEEN

Alberto Aguas

BACK IN THE EARLY 1980S, a woman came to my office and told me she had been guided to bring me a flyer about a world-famous healer from Brazil named Alberto Aguas. According to the flyer, he was coming to Minneapolis to teach a three-day workshop on healing. That same week, two more people came by the office with the same flyer. This definitely got my attention. I had heard people talk about this man and had read a book (*Psychic Healers*, by David St. Clair) that listed him as one of the world's most outstanding healers.

At that point, as far as I knew I was the only healer in Minneapolis doing laying-on-hands healing. I often worried that my clients weren't getting everything they needed from me because I'd never had any formal training; I had been taught only by spirit. The spirit of Jesus came to me often during healing sessions to instruct me. Native American spirits were also my teachers, as was the spirit of a Chinese-medicine doctor named Yang. These guides taught me about healing.

Another form of healing called Reiki was becoming popular in the Twin Cities, and many times I wondered if I should be taking classes on it. "No," my inner voice always said. I was getting everything I needed from my spirit teachers and the divine guidance within me.

The idea of being in the presence of another *living* healer who channeled laying-on-hands healing was exciting to me. I couldn't wait for Aguas to arrive. My inner voice was also excited. I could feel its affirming push to take the workshop. My only obstacle was that this was back in the early years of my self-employment as a psychic/ spiritual healer, when $80 was more than I could afford. I called my mom, and she agreed to lend me the money because she, too, had a strong sense that I should be in that class.

I had no logical reason to be anxious about calling to register but found I had to work up my nerve. When I did call, I asked the woman handling registrations if she thought there might be a chance Mr. Aguas would have lunch with me. I saw why I'd been apprehensive when she replied, "Well, now, if everyone who wanted to have lunch with Mr. Aguas actually did, he'd never have time for his work, would he?"

I hung up the phone, looked up to heaven, and asked God to please arrange some kind of meal with this healer so that I could pick his brain. After my prayer, I got a picture in my third eye of Mr. Aguas's address in the back of St. Clair's book. I went to my bookshelf, found the book, and nervously wrote a letter. I explained how excited I was about hearing him speak. If he had time, would he come to my house for dinner? I promised him a wonderful home-cooked meal. As I put the letter in the mail, I asked God to do whatever He could to make sure Mr. Aguas saw my note.

In addition to his three-day workshop, Aguas would be giving a talk at the Unity Church in nearby Golden Valley. I instructed all my students to attend.

A few years earlier I had attended a lecture on healing given by a healer in her late sixties. Also, an elderly male healer had given a sermon at my church. Because of these two healers, I expected Mr. Aguas to be up in age as well. With his reputation and experience, I thought he could be even older than they were.

Sunday morning at the Unity Church, with my mom and my students by my side, I waited excitedly for a stately old healer to enter the sanctuary and begin his talk. Instead, a man appeared who was so young and gorgeous that my jaw dropped. He had a beautiful tan, a full head of black hair, and deep brown eyes. He wore black pants and a lovely peach-colored sweater with half sleeves — the better to show off his muscular arms. I could barely look at him, he was so handsome! It was actually hard to concentrate on what he was saying unless I kept my head down and only peeked up once in a while. My soul was reacting so strongly that I couldn't wait for the service to end so I could leave.

Aguas finished his lecture with a beautiful meditation. Then the audience formed a line to shake his hand and thank him for his message, which was truly inspirational. He was so clearly filled with love for God and humankind; I wondered if I was worthy of meeting him.

I was so nervous that I got in and out of the line three times, and finally I was the only person left to greet him. I walked up, extended my hand, and looked him in the eye. Much to my surprise, *he* began to stammer. He quickly shook my hand and asked if I was coming to the workshop. I told him that I couldn't wait. He said, "Fine, I will see you there," and quickly disappeared. I thought about him for the rest of the day and couldn't sleep that night. I felt like my soul had found her mate.

The next night was day one of the workshop, and I was like a fourteen-year-old with a crush. I was all in a dither about what to wear. My spirit guide, John, who had never before shown any interest in my wardrobe, showed up and told me to wear my blue skirt and peach-colored sweater. This sweater was almost identical to the one Aguas had worn. John was so adamant about it that I knew I had to wear it. He even told me what jewelry to put on.

When I got to the workshop, the room was filled with twenty-nine women and three men. A woman recognized me from a recent newspaper article. We chatted for a bit, and I decided to sit with her and her daughter, Martha. The young woman asked if I was "into all this healing stuff." I told her it was my whole life, that I loved learning about healing and psychic abilities, and that my dream was to be a really good healer, like Aguas. I told her I was hoping to learn all the secrets about laying-on-hands healing from him. She laughed and said she had no desire to learn anything about healing, that she was just there to stare at Alberto for three days. He was that stunning.

When Alberto came into the room, I started to feel that inner anxiety again. I couldn't look at him very often. The energy between us felt so powerful, and these feelings were strange to me. They ran so deep. I felt a kind of intense spiritual connection that I didn't even know could exist.

Alberto was having a hard time making eye contact with me as well. When our eyes did meet, we would quickly dart them away. When class was over I made a beeline for the door. My feelings were too intense; I needed to get outside and breathe some fresh air.

I was walking to my car when a man from the workshop came running up to me. Mr. Aguas, he said, wanted to see me. "Me? Are you sure he wants to talk to me?" Spirit guide John told me to get in there and "act natural." My heart was pounding as I walked back into the room and asked Alberto if he wanted to see me. He said, in his very broken English, "Yes, Miss Bodi. I love that skirt and that beautiful sweater." His look melted me. I felt like I was in a scene from a movie — with the exception that John was standing there telling me to be cool. "Thank you, Mr. Aguas," I replied. "I'll see you tomorrow." To this, he said, "Oh, yes, darling, you will."

My soul did flip-flops that night. I felt so happy to have found this man, but at the same time it didn't feel like it was going to be easy knowing him. I had a sense, a kind of warning, that there was going to be a price to pay for the happiness I was feeling.

The next day, John again picked out my outfit: a pink skirt and white sweater, with a pink and blue necklace. As soon as Alberto entered the classroom, our eyes began their little dance. He was incredibly charming, and his accent was adorable. He was actually a bit hard to understand, but there was a magical, spiritual energy in the room that more than made up for this.

As soon as class ended, I headed out the door, and again someone from class came out to tell me that Alberto wanted to speak to me. Back in I went, with John by my side. Alberto told me I looked delightful in these beautiful clothes and asked if I would be coming back the next night. I told him I wouldn't miss it for anything, and he said, "Good night, Miss Bodi."

I was sad the next day because that night would be the last class. Alberto would be leaving to go back on the road at the end of the week. I feared I would never see him again, and this thought made me feel physically sick. John picked out an especially nice outfit for that evening, and I went to class with dozens of different feelings rolling around inside.

Throughout class, Alberto and I watched each other. I understood that expression about the "tension being so thick you could cut it with a knife." Nothing I tried to alleviate it was working. At break time, Alberto approached me where I was sitting with Martha and her mom.

"You got commitments?" he said.

"Excuse me?" I stammered.

"You got commitments?"

I thought I knew what he meant and asked, "Do you mean like a boyfriend, or a husband, or a family?"

He said, "Yes," and when I said, "No," he nodded his head. "Good. Then you travel with me. How many languages you speak?"

"One," I said.

"Hmm," he replied. "Okay. You want to go to dinner Friday night?"

Because his English was so broken, I thought I should make sure I wasn't just hearing what I *wanted* to hear. When I double-checked, he said, "Yes, Friday night. You pick me up? We go to Chez" — a very nice restaurant in a wealthy part of town. Then he told me he loved my outfit and said it was time to get back to work. I turned to Martha and her mom with a "what just happened here?" look. "Why not me?" Martha grinned. "What have you got that I don't?" We laughed so hard.

I couldn't concentrate on anything. All I could hear were the words *you travel with me*. It felt like a fairy tale, my own version of *Cinderella*: a world-renowned healer asking me to travel with him.

The dinner was magical. We talked more about doing healing work together and felt like we were the only people in the restaurant. The next day Alberto cancelled all his travel plans to stay in Minneapolis for another month. Each day when he finished his healing work, we would walk the lakes, holding hands and talking about everything under the sun. We had amazing conversations about God and healing. Every night we went to a different romantic restaurant. We so enjoyed just being with each other. It truly was a fairly tale.

On his last night in town, Alberto took me to a special restaurant for dinner. His mood was more somber than usual, and I assumed this was because he was leaving. We had talked about traveling together, but that wasn't diminishing the ache I felt inside. Now I understood the premonition I'd had that there was going to be an emotional price to pay for knowing this man.

We held hands at the restaurant and cried. After much conversation, we realized the feelings we had for each other were too difficult to sort through. He needed to travel and do his work, and I needed to stay in Minneapolis and do mine.

Over the next few years, we did travel together a few times, to various healing conventions. We were always in contact by phone, no matter where Alberto was in the world. We got very good at mental telepathy. We would send each other psychic messages and then verify them when we spoke by phone. Occasionally, when I hadn't seen him for a while, I had a conscious out-of-body experience and was able to visit him.

One day I got a whiff of Alberto's wonderful French cologne. I decided to lie down on my couch and ask my soul to visit him. I told her that I wanted to be conscious of the experience. Within seconds of asking, I/my soul was sitting in a dark movie theater. I looked around and saw Alberto, sitting down near the front with a female friend. When the movie was over, I followed him out of the theater. I needed to figure out where we were so that I could later confirm the experience with Alberto. I saw the word *cologne* and wondered if I was thinking about his perfume. I sent a thought to him, "Call me ASAP." Then my soul abruptly came back into my body.

Within a minute, the phone rang. Alberto said he was at a movie with a friend of his in Cologne, Germany, when he had a strong urge to call me. He was worried that something was wrong because the message came into his mind with such force. He couldn't believe it when I told him what had just happened. We marveled at the connection we shared.

Alberto's work took him all over the planet, and my work was focused here in Minneapolis. Over time our communication with each other dwindled.

In 1991 Alberto went to Brazil to visit his family. As always when he returned home, he visited the shamans in the Amazon jungle to learn more from them. Unfortunately, on this particular trip and unbeknownst to him, he caught malaria. When he came back to the States, he passed out at the New Jersey airport and ended up in quarantine for over a month. He was near death many times but always rallied. We made plans for him to come to Minneapolis for the summer. My intention was to channel healing to him and nurse him back to health.

At this same time, Alberto's mother became ill. He felt compelled to be with her in Brazil. His doctors advised against this, saying he would never survive the trip. But Alberto was devoted to his mother and wanted to be by her side. He died during his visit with her, on June 26, 1992.

Alberto's soul has come to visit me often, and I'm so grateful to be able to see him. He projects the smell of his cologne, and I hear his deep voice saying, "Hello, Bodi." Sometimes he appears when I'm channeling a healing, and sometimes he appears just because he can!

I learned so very much through this experience and from this wise and wonderful man. In the three-day workshop, I realized that God had shown me everything I needed to know to be a good healer. Alberto had learned about healing from the shamans in the Amazon; I had learned the same things from Jesus and other spirits. I was able to stop worrying that my clients weren't getting what they needed from me and felt even more grateful for the gift I'd been given.

With Alberto, I was able to experience the kind of love for someone that transcends the physical. I also learned about letting go of someone I badly wanted to be with. I saw that there is always a higher plan. I need to trust it rather than stay stuck on my own desired outcome.

I learned that love does not die when someone physically dies.

I almost forgot, and I bet you're wondering, too: Did he ever get my letter telling him I would make him a home-cooked meal? He did. This became one of the little jokes in our relationship once I realized my meatloaf and mashed potatoes weren't going to satisfy a man who loved spicy food. Almost daily, he would ask when I was going to prepare that meal I'd promised. I'd always say, "Tomorrow." In our last telephone conversation, I told him he'd be getting many a home-cooked meal when he came here to heal. We both giggled.

(You can see pictures of this very lovely man on my website, www.echobodine.com.)

FOR YOU TO THINK ABOUT

Looking for the Good in Your Love Relationships

Have you ever wanted to be with someone so much that your body ached? Did it feel as if every part of you had finally met your soul mate but that it was impossible for the two of you to be together?

If you have, I'd like you to write about your experience in

your journal. It's important for us to acknowledge the hurt and pain we go through when something like this happens. If we don't, that grief eats away at us. We can have all kinds of physical and emotional problems as a result. We can also begin to blame God if the relationship doesn't work out as we hoped, but it's not God's fault.

Write out all the details that you can remember, and then go outside for a walk. Get out in nature, where your body can feel grounded, and walk for as long as you can. When you come back from your walk, go back to your journal. This time, write down all the reasons it was good that the relationship didn't work. You may not want to do this, but it's important. Do it for the sake of your health and so that you can move on from the hurt. I guarantee, if the two of you were meant to be together, you would have been. If being with that person were for your highest good, you would have been.

As I'm writing, an image from *The Wizard of Oz* pops into my mind. Just as in that film, so much of life goes on "behind the scenes." Some of the "whys" hide behind a curtain; we don't have the whole picture.

The last night that Alberto was in town, we both cried in the restaurant because we knew our paths were meant to separate. We had one amazing month together, a month that strengthened both of us, but it was not meant to last a lifetime. Alberto taught me about a different kind of love, and this healed me in ways I didn't expect. I was able to look for the good in my relationship with Alberto, and when I did, I saw God everywhere.

CHAPTER SEVENTEEN

Heroes

I DEFINE HEROES as people with true humility who go out on a limb and show the rest of us what is possible. One of my heroes was psychic medium James Van Praagh. As far back as I can remember, I've loved watching him work. Whenever he was on television, my friends would call to make sure I knew he was on. I would stay glued to the screen, watching everything he did. His gifts amazed me. I often commented to my mom that I wished I were as talented.

Summer 2000 was coming to an end, when I got a call from my friend Gary Beckman, the owner of a local alternative newspaper called *The Edge*. He told me that James was coming to the Twin Cities in September and asked if I would be interested in interviewing him for their newspaper. He thought that one psychic interviewing another would be a fresh slant for the story.

"Yes!" I screamed into the phone. I was so excited. Not only was I going to meet James Van Praagh in person, but I was going to get to ask him a bunch of questions. This was a dream come true.

What should I wear? What should I ask him? How was I going to calm myself down so that I didn't come across as a crazed fan?

Fortunately, I learned that two girlfriends of mine would be working with James during his visit, one coordinating his media and the other escorting him from one engagement to the next. The three of us planned to do the interview at a very nice restaurant in nearby Edina called Ciao Bella.

The night before James came to town, I was so excited I couldn't sleep. I'd picked out five different outfits to wear, gotten a manicure and pedicure, colored my hair, and rewritten the interview questions at least a dozen times. I wanted everything to be perfect.

The next morning, I tried on each of the outfits. Should I be respectful and wear a dress? Should I look professional and wear a business suit? Were slacks okay? I didn't want to be overdressed or underdressed. As I've learned to do, I eventually trusted my intuition to pick out the outfit, and off to lunch I went.

From Ciao Bella, I checked in with my girlfriends via cell phone to make sure there were no glitches. James was doing several interviews that morning with our local television stations, and they were on their way to the restaurant. "How are you holding up?" asked one of my friends. "I'm a nervous wreck," I replied. Then James grabbed my friend's phone and said, "Get a grip, or we aren't coming!" I was speechless. I sat there with my mouth open and realized I really did need to get a grip because I was going to make an absolute fool of myself if I didn't.

Even before I saw them, I could tell that they had arrived, because the energy in the restaurant changed. It was as if everyone in the room had perked up a notch. They sat down at the table, I was introduced, and there I was, face-to-face with my hero. (He's quite handsome, with the longest eyelashes and the most beautiful blue eyes. . . .)

I tried hard not to act like a nerdy fan. We ordered lunch, and James mentioned that my friends had told him I had psychic abilities. He asked what kind of readings I did and how long I had been doing them. They had also told him about the books I'd written and some of the publicity I'd had. I felt squirmy, like I wanted to get the conversation off me and back onto him. I felt a huge responsibility to the newspaper to get a good interview, so I asked if he wouldn't mind if I proceeded with my questions while he ate lunch. (My stomach was in such a knot there was no way I could eat.)

I asked the usual questions — When had he discovered his gift? How had he developed his abilities? I then asked him how his work affected his health. This grabbed James's attention. "I've never been asked that question before," he said. He looked at me intently for a long moment — with those big baby blues — and then said, "You tell me."

I stammered, "Excuse me?"

"Read me, babe," he replied.

My heart jumped into my throat. "You want *me* to give *you* a reading?" He gestured with his hand as if to say, "Go ahead; do it."

My blood pressure must have shot up over 200 right at that moment. I really thought I was going to start hyperventilating. As soon as I had the thought "God, help!" a very nice female spirit floated up to me and said, "Don't worry, sweetie, I'll help you with this." She identified herself as James's deceased mom.

I closed my eyes and felt a calmness come over me. I focused completely on his mother's words and gave them to James, word for word. Other spirits joined in and gave me information to share with him. It was actually fun. The spirits addressed several areas of James's life, including how his work affected his health.

One of my friends interrupted me to say that James needed to get going to his next interview. I thanked his mother and other spirit friends and opened my eyes to find James sitting there looking quite flabbergasted. The first words out of his mouth were, "How did you do that?" He then told me I was very accurate and that he was impressed. He asked me if I was busy that evening and if not, would I like to accompany him to Barnes & Noble, where he was doing a book-signing. He thought that we could sign our books together. Then he asked if I would like to join him afterward for a spot he was doing on *Entertainment Tonight*. And before he left, he told me he would do whatever he could to help further my career.

I left the restaurant on top of the world. I called the woman in charge of signings at Barnes & Noble and told her that James had suggested we both come that night to sign our books together. I'll never forget what she said: there was no way the store could handle the crowd that James and I would pull in together.

I did attend James's book-signing, and afterward I accompanied him to the taping for *Entertainment Tonight*, where we worked together on the case of a missing girl. It was a special day, and I came away feeling so blessed.

All my life I've compared myself to others and always thought that they were more talented, better looking, smarter. Whenever I had seen James on television doing his readings, I had been discouraged with my own development as a psychic because I wasn't doing mediumship at the same level.

Doing that reading for James at lunch and then working with him on the missing person case was very liberating. I realized I *had* developed my abilities very well. I was at a level I should be proud of. There was no reason to feel discouraged about my abilities. It was very clear to me that night that I needed to stop comparing myself to others and that I could and should be proud of myself for the commitment I had made to developing my gifts.

When the woman at Barnes & Noble said that there was no way the store could handle doing a book-signing for both of us at the same time, it hit me: she was putting me in the same category as James. I felt like a part of me arrived that day, and I was so grateful that I hadn't given up along the way. Developing abilities takes time and dedication. They do not come overnight. I felt proud for working hard and trusting that I was on the right path. And I felt a tremendous amount of love and gratitude to God for pushing me as hard as He did. He doesn't need two James Van Praaghs. He needs one James, one Echo — and one *you*.

FOR YOU TO THINK ABOUT

Do You Have Heroes?

Do you compare yourself to others? Does it seem like other people get the breaks and you don't? Do you secretly feel that God has it out for you and that's why the other guy gets the good stuff?

Comparing ourselves to others can be useful in that others can show us what is possible. James Van Praagh is an excellent medium, and without him, the general public would know much less about the subject. But comparing can also *keep us small* if we are always seeing the other guy, or gal, as better-off than we are. We have to be careful not to use this as a cop-out, a way to keep ourselves from striving for more.

Are there people in your life you compare yourself to? Is this getting in the way of your moving forward? Have you ever wondered why you do it? Is there a payoff in making yourself small?

Answer these questions in your journal. Be very honest with yourself; I've found that comparing is a common way of staying stuck, and this journaling could help you move forward.

I have a brother who is a very gifted artist. I used to compare myself to him all the time. I couldn't draw a circle unless I traced a bowl, so for years I gave up the idea of being creative. One day it dawned on me that I might not be a great artist like my brother, but I could probably do some kind of craft. I took a candle-making class at a local hobby shop, and it opened up a whole new world for me.

Pay attention to the heroes in your life. What are they doing that you aren't doing? What skills do they have that you think you don't have?

If they have a skill that you admire, figure out if there's a way you can cultivate that skill, or, better yet, start focusing on the things you can already do. We *all* have gifts and talents, and it's such a waste of time to think we might as well not bother because others are more advanced.

This is your life, and *you* need to make the most of it.

Also, think of the heroes in your life and make a list in your journal of all the qualities you like in them. Then walk away from the list for a few days, and when you go back to it, try to look at the list from a more objective perspective. I bet you'll see that you have many of these qualities yourself, buried somewhere. You would not recognize and gravitate toward those qualities unless you also had them on some level.

We tend to make others out to be more powerful, more talented, and more gifted out of fear — fear of recognition, fear of failure, *and* fear of success. We play the victim by saying "Poor me. Nothing good ever happens to me," but the truth is, we have two choices every day of our lives: we can choose to be the victim, or we can choose to be the victor. Good can be found in any situation if we look for it, and every situation in your life can be turned around with effort.

You are an amazing human being. You have talents and gifts you've probably never tapped into. Remember that your life is an adventure and that you are the main character in it. Ask God to show you your gifts and talents — and be your own hero.

CHAPTER EIGHTEEN

First Book Published

WRITERS HOPING TO GET PUBLISHED often ask me what process I went through to get my first book published. I'm almost embarrassed to tell them, because compared to some of the horror stories I've heard from other authors about getting turned down over and over again, my story is another example of trusting and acting on inner guidance.

Back in the early 1980s, my inner voice told me to write a very simple book about spiritual healing. It said that some people were getting too intellectual about the subject, overanalyzing and complicating it.

But writing a book seemed impossible. I haven't had any formal training in writing — though I do remember my spirit guides telling me to pay attention in college English. (They had to nudge me because my tendency was to drift off!) When I got the book idea, my guides told me not to worry and assured me that they'd help me with the project, which they did. Every few days, just before I woke up, they would tell me a subject I needed to write about. By the end of six weeks, I had a thirty-page manuscript. At the time, this seemed as big an accomplishment as writing *War and Peace*.

I knew that the next step was to turn the manuscript in to a publisher, but there was no way I wanted to put myself through that. I was sure the book would be turned down, and I didn't think I had the heart to handle the rejection. So I stuck the pages on a shelf and waited for the courage to take the next step.

One night, as I was leaving home to meet my friend Lynne Burmyn for dinner, my inner voice told me to show her the manuscript, since she is a published author. When I did, Lynne said I should definitely show my work to a publisher. I told her I'd think about it, knowing full well I wasn't going to do anything that scary. Still, it felt great that Lynne thought it was worth a shot. She also said she wanted to go through the manuscript more slowly and asked if she could take it home. "Fine by me," I said. As the weeks passed, I got busy doing other things and pretty much forgot she even had it.

Then, one day, an envelope came that looked like junk mail. I tossed it in the garbage but totally out of the blue came a resounding "Read that letter" from my inner voice. I went back to the garbage and retrieved the letter to find that it was from ACS Publications in San Diego, California. It said that if the manuscript were longer, they would consider it for publication.

I actually called the woman who had written the letter to see if this was a joke. She said no, it wasn't a joke, and that they had very much enjoyed what I'd written. But, she said, "We need a hundred more pages. Why not put in some of the healing experiences you've had with clients over the years?"

I was absolutely flabbergasted. Here was pure acceptance, without first having to go through any of the rejection I was so afraid of.

When I called Lynne to thank her, she was just as excited. She said her inner voice had told her to send the manuscript to her publisher and that she'd had a strong feeling they would go for it.

It took another three months for me to finish the manuscript, but when I turned it in, ACS was very pleased with the additions. They published the book in 1985, and *Hands That Heal* has stayed in print ever since. In 2002 ACS gave me back the rights, and New World Library bought it. We updated the information and put on a beautiful new cover, and the book is still selling very well.

Speaking of books, I'd like to share another story about courage and timing. When I'd written my third book — which I called *The Truth about Ghosts* but later was called *Echoes of the Soul* — my inner voice kept prompting me to send the manuscript to Marc Allen, the cofounder and publisher of New World Library. I knew someone who knew him personally, so I asked her to take a look at the book and pass it on to Marc if she thought he would like it. This woman emailed me about two weeks later saying that she loved the book and thought that Marc would, too. She said she would hand-deliver it to him and that I should give Marc a few weeks to go over it because he was a very busy man.

I waited and waited and heard nothing. One Saturday night while sitting at my desk, I prayed for the courage to call Marc and leave a voice mail introducing myself. I thought this would be a good way to break the ice — and spur Marc to call me back.

Because it was a Saturday night, I didn't expect Marc to answer the phone, but that's exactly what he did. I was stunned. I started talking really fast, introducing myself and my book, and going on and on about how we could actually turn it into two books instead of one, and how I knew the title was kind of goofy but we could change that, until finally, I ran out of words. Then, instead of Marc saying what every writer dreams of hearing, something like, "I loved your book, you are a fantastic writer, and I can't wait to publish it," he said, "Who *are* you and what are you talking about?" He and I still laugh about the conversation.

Yes, I got up the courage, and yes, I did make a little bit of a fool of myself, but Marc never forgot that phone call and has gone on to publish the majority of my books.

When we want something and it's the right thing for us, God will help us in many ways. Conversely, if we want something and face roadblocks or rejection, "No" isn't necessarily a bad thing. If we hang in there for a bit, we'll usually see why the roadblocks were there. Here's an example of what I mean.

When the movie *The Sixth Sense* was doing well at the box office, I got a call from the people at the television show *The View*. They wanted to talk to a psychic about the movie and asked if I could fly to New York the next day. They said they were choosing between me and a psychic from New York. They'd get back to me by the end of the day with their decision.

I was so excited I could hardly breathe. I called my publisher. I called all my friends. I asked God to please make sure they chose me and waited all day by the phone for the call that never came.

The next morning I called *The View*'s producer. He said they'd decided to go with the New York psychic so that they wouldn't have to pay airfare. I was so bummed out! I couldn't understand why God hadn't made this happen.

The next day, the segment aired, and I saw why I hadn't been chosen. The hosts of the show were very hard on the young male psychic. They treated him disrespectfully, and it made me quite angry. If they had been that way with me, I don't know how I would have handled it. But the psychic — John Edward — was clearly the right man for the job; he handled it all beautifully. I had never heard of John (this was before his own show was on the air), but as someone in the field, I was tremendously proud of the way he presented himself. It was crystal clear to me that I was being protected and that John was where he was meant to be.

FOR YOU TO THINK ABOUT

What Do You Need to Do to Make Your Dreams Come True?

Are you afraid to try something for fear of failure? Is there a half-finished project sitting in the back of your closet? An invention you've created or a screenplay collecting dust under the bed?

As you've just read, I was terrified of being turned down. My project sat on a shelf for months before I had the courage to show it to Lynne. It takes guts to present our ideas to the "experts." They might laugh us right out of their office — but then again, they might just invite us to sign a contract.

Also, when someone else gets what we think we wanted, we need to remember that we don't know what's going on behind the scenes. If life seems to say no to you, life is probably protecting you from something. Life will say yes when the time is right.

If an idea for a project has been rolling around in your head for the past few years but you've been afraid to attempt it, go for it. Ask for guidance and then practice listening to your intuition rather than your fear. Take the first small step that could get your plan or project rolling. What's the worst that could happen?

If "the worst" does happen — you aren't chosen or the person on the other end of the line isn't receptive — consider this as part of the plan.

Write in your journal about your dream goal, and then each day, ask your inner voice what you need to do that day to make your goals come true.

When we have a dream that doesn't go away, I believe it's God's way of telling us to create it. If you need courage, ask God to lend you some. Ask for the right people to come into your life so that you can make your dream a reality. Then pay attention to all the signs along the way. Listen to your dreams, and act on them. You don't want to leave this lifetime with regrets, do you?

CHAPTER NINETEEN

IRS

YOU MIGHT BE SURPRISED to find a chapter on the Internal Revenue Service in a book about spiritual growth. But it's through our challenges that most of us grow spiritually — and I think we'd all agree that the IRS often presents a challenge.

Being self-employed is great in many ways. I can stay in my pajamas all day and do a lot of my work from home. I can take two hours for lunch and not worry about a cranky boss looking over my shoulder. If I want to make personal phone calls, I can. If I need a break from the world, I can walk away from the phones and go out in my garden.

Being self-employed also has its challenges. The area that's been most challenging for me over the years is staying current on income taxes. It's so easy to put the money back into the business or to use it for bills.

There always seem to be unexpected expenses, like needing a new washing machine or a car repair. It's easy to dip into the money that you've set aside for taxes when the cat needs to go to the vet or business is slow for a month and you don't have enough money to pay the mortgage. We may intend to put the money back into the tax account ASAP but, well, life happens — and the money disappears.

My tax problems started when I had four major surgeries in two years *without* health insurance. I was totally overwhelmed, with thousands of dollars in medical bills. Bills turned into notices from bill collectors and then from collection agencies. I got phone calls every day from people (some nice, some not so nice) wanting money.

I spent so many hours berating myself for not making more money and for not being smarter with the money I did make. I felt terrible shame about not being a "responsible citizen." As each year passed, the mess got worse.

It was everything I could do to keep my head above water and the bill collectors at bay. Then letters started coming from the IRS and the State of Minnesota, reminding me that interest and penalties were piling up on my past-due tax payments. They were going to start proceedings to levy my bank accounts and put liens on my property. I ended up getting audited.

I was a nervous wreck in the days leading up to the audit. Once the female auditor got to my home and I saw how nice she was, something in me started to shift. I realized she was not a monster, here to take my house away, but a woman doing her job and trying to help me get back on track. I was surprised at how much my attitude changed by the time the audit was over.

I found that the State of Minnesota was a lot tougher about collecting money than the federal government. Randomly, they would go into my checking account and take out whatever money was there. And they always seemed to know when I had just deposited a significant amount. (Someone at the bank later told me they were instructed to let the State know when I had deposited a large sum.) I can't tell you how sick to my stomach I felt every time I made a deposit and wondered if the money would be gone by the end of the day. It was awful.

I hit bottom before things started to turn around. I can laugh at the experience today, but at the time there was *nothing* to laugh about.

It was late in summer. The Minnesota State Fair was going on, and I loved going to the fair. The year before, I'd been so financially strapped I hadn't been able to buy anything other than a few corn dogs at the fair. I vowed that I would make it up to myself the following year by tucking away a little money here and there before the fair came to town. I had managed to save $100 and was so looking forward to going.

A few days before my scheduled day at the fair, I deposited a large check into my checking account, fees for a speaking engagement. I used the money to write out several doctor's bills. I mailed out all the checks and was feeling good about keeping the bill collectors off my back for another month. This was on a Thursday, and as soon as I finished with my last client of the day, I was headed out to the fair.

As I was literally walking out the door, my bank called to say that the State had just taken all the money out of my account. Not only was I completely broke, but all the checks to the doctors were going to bounce. Plus, oh yeah, there was a $30 fee for every bounced check. I walked into the kitchen, grabbed a bag of chocolate chips, stuffed a handful in my mouth, and started crying like a baby. I felt totally defeated. I had been doing the best I could, and it wasn't working.

I really didn't think things could get any worse. Then the doorbell rang. I was crying so hard I thought about not answering it, but it rang again. With my tear-stained chocolaty face, I answered the door and found a woman holding up a badge. She introduced herself as an agent from the IRS, there to look over my finances.

In one very long sentence and without taking a breath, I told her that the State of Minnesota had just levied my checking account. I was going to have several overdrafts. I was completely broke. And I wasn't going to be able to go to the fair. Then, with tears streaming down my face, I handed her the bag of chocolate chips and asked her if she wanted any.

The agent turned out to be a very nice person. She sat with me and calmed me down. We had a very good talk, and she reassured me that she would work with me to find a solution. This was a turning point for me. I knew I had to handle my finances differently — and that didn't mean getting another credit card or trying to get a loan.

It was about turning all this over to God. It was about asking God for help every time another collection letter came. It was about praying for the right words when calling the State to get the levy reversed. I was so cloaked in shame for not paying my taxes that I'd gotten stuck. I needed a different approach mentally, emotionally, and spiritually — and God was it.

The IRS agent laid out a step-by-step plan for me to follow that would eventually lead me to make an Offer in Compromise. (Based on your income, they will accept a one-time settlement if you can prove for two years that you are going to stay current on your estimated taxes.) I also started praying for guidance every time I had to make any contact with the IRS or the State. I would pray for the right words when talking to them and would always ask God to let me know when the timing was perfect for making the phone call. A few times after receiving nasty, threatening letters, I made calls without checking in with my intuition. Both times I got "agents from hell." One of them said she was only going to let me eat rice and beans until I got the bill paid up; the other one wasn't even going to let me have that.

But when I made a call at the urging of my inner voice, the person on the other end of the phone was always an angel. She or he knew that I was trying to run a business, that I wasn't taking expensive vacations or buying luxury boats, that my car was twelve years old, and that I didn't have assets other than my home (which they had several liens on). It was clear I wasn't trying to con anyone.

My inner voice was also clear about not running any scams. Whenever anyone suggested that I hide my money or not deposit any cash, my intuition was adamant about being honest and up-front *always*. When I got a call or letter that triggered my fear or shame, the toughest thing was calming myself down and focusing only on the still, small voice within. Over time, and with practice tuning in to this voice, I got to the point that I could tell which letters were computer-generated mass mailings and which ones were important to pay close attention to.

It was a fascinating lesson in learning to let go of fear and in not giving up all my power. Yes, they did have the power to take away anything they wanted. But I had the power to decide what was and wasn't important. Were my material possessions more important than my peace of mind? No. Peace of mind and good health were more important than anything I owned. I came to see that for my sanity, I had to look at this whole relationship with the IRS as a blessing rather than a curse. I had to learn as much from it as I could. As the situation continued to heal, I realized that the IRS had brought me closer to God because I was finally giving God — not the IRS — the power.

Every once in a while, I'd backslide. I'd get into my humanness and try to control things. I would pray, for instance, to be shown ways to make more money. God would just continue teaching me to:

- stop reacting from fear and shame
- see the collectors and agents as regular human beings doing their jobs and treat them the way I wanted to be treated and not as mean, all-powerful monsters
- stop giving those I owed money more power than God; God is ultimately in charge and uses my inner voice to tell me exactly how to handle situations
- take responsibility, rather than blaming "them"
- look to the future with the belief that all would be well, rather than wallowing in self-pity (or chocolate chips!)

As I became more and more committed to doing whatever was necessary, the pieces continued to fall into place. The hard lessons weren't over yet. I still had to learn more about letting go and trusting. The most painful experience was that I had to sell my house and give the IRS all the proceeds. But this got them off my back once and for all. The second toughest experience was that I needed to move in with my boyfriend, which was difficult for this very independent woman. An incredible amount of good came from that also.

Eventually, I got all the medical bills paid up, got current on my estimated taxes for two years, and made an Offer in Compromise to the IRS that was accepted. I also became very good friends with the agent at the State of Minnesota who kept levying my account!

The story had many happy endings including this one:

One night about five years after I sold my house, my assistant and I were driving home from a book-signing. My inner voice told me to drive by my former house to show my assistant where I used to live. I didn't want to get sad — I had loved that house so much — but my inner voice urged me again, so I drove by.

There on the front lawn was a "For Sale" sign. My inner voice said, "Now you can have your house back."

I was so excited I barely slept a wink that night. Was it possible? Could I really buy it back? I had no money to put down, my credit rating was still healing, and yet something inside kept telling me to go for it.

As soon as I woke up, I called the realtor and told her I was the former owner and wanted to buy the house back. She said the house had been on the market for over a year. No one could believe it wasn't selling. She said the owners had tried everything. When I called, she said she knew the house was simply waiting for me.

Once again, the pieces fell into place, and I was able to buy the house back. (Go to my website, www.echobodine.com, to see a picture of it.)

FOR YOU TO THINK ABOUT

Who's All-Powerful in Your Life?

Do you have similar issues with someone or something powerful? It could be the IRS or bill collectors, but it could also be an abusive family member, a domineering boss, or a spouse.

Some people love to intimidate. It's important for all of us to remember that these people have power *only if we give it to them*. We have to stay clear that no matter what they do, we will stay focused on our spiritual path and remember that *God* is the one with the real power.

If you are being hassled by someone like this, are you losing sleep over it? Is it affecting your health or causing depression? Has it made you think about suicide?

I hate to think of your "yes" answers but know firsthand what they feel like. I went through all of the above during my experience with the IRS. But when I started asking God for help, I began to feel my intuition guiding me and started to see the light at the end of the tunnel.

So much of it has to do with reaching out for help. First go to God. Ask Him for guidance about who to turn to for help. Then trust your inner nudges and make those phone calls.

TAKE LIFE ONE DAY AT A TIME

I have another suggestion for you, one that has helped me tremendously through the years: "Take one day at a time."

AA is full of one-liner slogans: Easy Does It, Live and Let Live, Keep It Simple — and One Day at a Time.

The first three were easy to incorporate into my life, but living one day at a time just didn't seem realistic when I was a woman in my twenties. I was always projecting into the future, always living for that illusive "someday" when everything would be great. But I had a very cool sponsor in the program who worked to keep my feet firmly planted on the ground.

Getting a medallion for significant days of sobriety is a very big deal in AA, and my one-year sobriety date was coming up. I was so excited about getting that medallion because it had been a long year of many, many changes.

The meeting where I wanted to get my medallion met on Monday nights, and my one-year anniversary date was on Tuesday. I asked my sponsor if he would give me my medallion one day early. He looked at me almost in disgust. He was a stickler for living one day at a time, so there was no way he was giving me that medallion on Monday when my anniversary was Tuesday. My anniversary hadn't arrived yet. What was I thinking? I was thinking that my sponsor was being way too rigid.

Shortly after this, my minister gave a sermon on the Lord's Prayer. He said that when we ask God to give us our daily bread we are asking that our daily needs be met. He pointed out that the prayer doesn't say weekly, monthly, or yearly. It says *daily*, which ties in completely with living one day at a time.

Realistically, all we have is today. If you think about it, even making it through a whole day isn't guaranteed. When we stop living in the future — or in the past — we realize that we have right now, in this very moment, all we need to handle right now. This eliminates so much of what stresses, frightens, depresses, and shames us.

Have you ever tried living in the now? It takes discipline. It's not easy, because we're so used to counting on the future. I really want you to practice living in the present for a few days. See for yourself how much easier life gets. Learn how long an hour is. See how much you can accomplish in fifteen minutes. Once you start living in the now, time becomes precious and you make good use of it.

See if this doesn't make a big difference in your life and in the way you handle your version of the IRS.

CHAPTER TWENTY

Healing a Phobia

ONE OF MY CONSTANT PRAYERS for many years was "Please help me to be a wonderful healer." I had such an ache in my heart to be the best healer I could possibly be, and as you've seen, I've had some truly amazing experiences with this gift. One thing I haven't yet described is how parts of *me* have healed in the process of working on others. Here's an example.

As far back as I can remember, I've had a terrible fear of fire. When I was little, I was even afraid when my parents made a fire in the fireplace. I'd sit way across the room and make sure no one got too close to it. If my dad and brother were wrestling in front of the fire, I'd have to leave the room because I was so terrified one of them would be burned. As I got older, whenever anything came on TV about burn victims, I'd quickly change the channel. I could *feel* the pain they were in and smell their burned flesh. If I or someone I knew got burned, I suffered needless anxiety about it and felt claustrophobic. It was a heavy issue for me.

One day a woman came in for a healing. My assistant set up all my appointments, so I had no idea what kind of help this woman was seeking. As she was walking up to my door, I noticed that her face looked strange. As she got closer to the door, I realized she had a clear mask on her face. She was a burn victim.

I immediately started to hyperventilate and didn't think I'd be able to answer the door. I honestly felt frozen with fear at the thought of having to look at her. As she rang my doorbell, I sent out a heartfelt prayer — "Oh, my God, help me." This calmed me some, but I was still very anxious.

The woman came in and took off her mask. She explained that she had been in a house fire and that it had burned her entire face and her arms. I was absolutely terrified to look her in the face, and yet I had to. I didn't want her to feel bad or take my fear personally. When I did look at her face, I saw that she had no eyebrows or lashes, and that her nose had not healed completely; there was a hole on the side of it. Her lips had been burned off. Her hair was gone, and she had several different colors of skin on her face. It looked like a patchwork quilt of brown, pink, and white.

The woman's arms were one big mass of scar tissue. I doubted I would be able to channel healing to her because I was feeling so claustrophobic. But then something inside me took over. A power, a calmness, and an inner strength that I can only call my Higher Self came to the surface. I had her lie down on my healing table, and I put hankies on all the areas I was going to work on.

Healing energy poured out of my hands, and I wondered what the energy would be able to do. The healing lasted for about forty-five minutes, and when the woman left, she said she wanted to see how things went and that she'd call me if she wanted another appointment.

Two weeks later, she called for another appointment, and

though I was again nervous beforehand, I felt more ready to see her this time. When she came in, she removed her mask and I saw a marked improvement. Her nose had healed back to normal. Her eyebrows, hair, and eyelashes were coming in nicely. And the patches on her skin were blending together. She said that her doctor was amazed at how well she was progressing.

I channeled another very intense healing, and when she left, she again said she'd call if she needed another. I noticed then that something inside *me* was healing because I was so much less afraid to be around her.

In another two weeks, the woman came back to see me. This time there was no mask. Instead, a beautiful woman came to my door. I didn't recognize her. The skin on her face was all one color, and it was as fresh and healthy as a baby's. Her hair was growing in quickly. She had mascara on her eyelashes and lipstick on her full, healthy lips. She was really very pretty. The scars on her arms were gone as well. Her doctors, she said, could not believe the healing she had experienced.

We knew this was the last time we would see each other. She was moving back up north to rebuild her house. We hugged good-bye and held on to each other for a bit. She wasn't the only one who had received healing. I had healed from my anxiety and claustrophobia about fire and burns. I was so grateful to God for how He had helped me overcome this terrible phobia that had plagued me for so long.

FOR YOU TO THINK ABOUT

Helping Others Helps You

Can you recall a time when you helped another person and felt helped yourself? A time when you received as you gave?

Most of us feel good when we know we've been of service. But there's often more to it than that. We may not be aware of the ways we are being helped — or even healed — in the moment. We may only notice this aspect after the fact. Perhaps our act of giving or helping was hard on us physically, emotionally, or financially. We might have had to push ourselves and call on inner reserves.

But then, on reflection, we see what we've been given — a sense of our strength and ability, an awareness of God working through us and with us. Reflect on this and write about it in your journal. Give and you shall receive.

CHAPTER TWENTY-ONE

Finding My Baby

I WROTE EARLIER about giving a baby up for adoption when I was a young, single woman. This was, of course, a very significant event in my life. Its significance didn't end back then.

From the day "my baby" turned eighteen, every year on his birthday I'd ask God if it would be okay to start looking for him. I always got the same inner sense: wait.

There were times when I would agonize about it and other times when I would trust divine timing. I had such a deep longing to find him and know everything about him. Signing the adoption papers, giving up all rights to him, didn't break the connection I felt. He was my child. He came out of my body. I wanted to have a relationship with him in whatever form he was comfortable with. It was something I had to do, but I knew the timing had to be right. As I've always tried to do, I left it in God's hands and simply asked Him to let me know when I could act.

It was June 1993, four months before my son's twenty-fifth

birthday, when I woke up to a male voice saying, "You can start looking for your son."

I flew out of bed. "Did you just say I can start looking for my baby?" I asked God. I got an inner nudge — *yes*. When I asked Him how I was to go about doing this, my inner voice said I would know later that day.

I ran to my appointment book to see if anything special was happening. I saw that I had four clients coming in for healing. Knowing God a bit by now, I figured one of those four people would provide the next piece to the puzzle.

When I asked my fourth client of the day what she would like healing for, she told me that she was adopted and had just located her birth parents.

She said she was going through quite a bit of emotional turmoil around it but that, all in all, it was a great experience. I sat there with my mouth open, fixed on every word she said. I asked her how she had found them, and she said that she had hired an agency in California. These people could get past any closed records. When my client got home that night, she called and left the number of the woman who owned this agency on my phone machine.

I sat staring at that number all night. This woman, whose name and number I was holding in my hand, could actually find my baby for me.

I called Doreen the very next morning, and she was an absolute delight to talk to. She had been adopted herself and was now helping others find their birth parents. She told me that she would send me some papers to fill out and that the fee was $500 — $300 now and $200 when she found my boy. Her parting words to me were, "I'll have your baby for you in two to six weeks."

I was pretty much a basket case for the rest of that day. My dream was becoming a reality. I was finally going to meet the son I had put up for adoption twenty-five years earlier.

The only hitch was that I didn't have $300. I had no extra money at all and no idea where I could get any. I asked God for help, and my inner knowing said it would all be fine.

Four days later (on the same day, in fact, that I learned Alberto had died), I found three items in my mailbox — papers to start the agency search, a check for $75 from a client paying for a past reading, and a check for $225, an unexpected insurance rebate. There in my hands were the papers and the $300.

I was intuitively guided to find things to occupy my time while Doreen was conducting the search. I bought a few books about birth children reuniting with their birth parents, and I devoured them. I talked to the social worker at Children's Home Society here in the Twin Cities, who had helped my father find his birth family. She and the books helped me know what I should expect. Sons, for instance, are more apt than daughters to want to be in control of the meeting. They may choose not to meet their birth parents for a variety of reasons — they don't want to upset their adoptive parents, they don't feel settled in their own lives, they want more time before meeting. They might also be angry at their birth parents for placing them for adoption, and in some cases, they may not know they were adopted.

Weeks passed, and Doreen was having a hard time locating my son in California, where he was born. I was surprised to find myself somewhat relieved. The reality of it all was hitting me with each book I read and each conversation I had. I was becoming afraid that he might not want to meet me. What if he slammed that door shut, as had happened in some of the stories I'd read? I had to be ready for that possibility but didn't want to think about it.

August 10 was a sad day for me because I had to have my dog

put down that morning. He had been suffering from a rare disease for several years, and though healings had kept him in remission for a while, the disease was now back with a vengeance and it was clearly his time.

I remember walking back from the vet's office that morning and asking God, "Is there any way I can get some information about my son?" Five minutes after I got home, the phone rang. It was Doreen — with good news. She hadn't located my son yet, but she knew his name. She told me to grab a sheet of paper, sit down, and take a few breaths.

For those of you who haven't been through a situation like this, finding out your child's name might seem insignificant. I'll tell you, it was quite overwhelming. Doreen said that the next time I heard from her, she would be able to tell me where he lived. I must have stared at his name for the rest of the night. Kurt, with a "K." It sounded so strong.

It took Doreen two more months to locate Kurt. His family had moved back to Nebraska, where his father was from, and she had been searching for him on the West Coast.

She and I talked at great length the afternoon she gave me Kurt's number. She coached me on what to say and then told me to let her know how our first meeting went. She said to verify that his birthday was correct because there were two people listed in Lincoln with his name.

I could barely sleep that night. I tossed and turned. I rehearsed my speech over and over. I called my mother a hundred times for reassurance that I was doing the right thing. I called my son's birth father to let him know what was happening. (We'd kept in touch over the years.)

Morning finally came, and it was time to make the phone call.

The first time I called, a young woman answered the phone and said that Kurt had just left for the grocery store. She said he would be back in twenty minutes. I told her I wasn't sure I had the right person and wanted to confirm that his birthday was November 20, 1968. Yes, she said, that was his date of birth. I told her I would call back in twenty minutes. Then I sat down and started to cry. Anxiety had built up to the point where I thought I was going to explode. Once again I doubted I had the strength to go through with this, so I reached out and asked God to hold my hand and share some of His courage with me.

Twenty minutes passed. I dialed the number and hung up three times before letting it ring. Finally, on the fourth time, I let it ring and the same young woman answered. She said that Kurt was home from the store and that she'd get him. A few moments later, a young man's voice said, "Hello."

"Is this Kurt?" I asked.

"Yes."

"Were you born in Mountain View, California, on November 20, 1968?"

"Yes."

"Do you know that you're adopted?"

Again I heard, "Yes."

Then, following the script Doreen had provided, I asked if he had time for a very personal phone call.

"Well, that depends on what you've got to say," he replied.

With that, I took a deep breath, told him my name, and said I believed I was his birth mother.

About five seconds later, Kurt said "This is my mom? You're my mom?" His next question was about his father: What did he look like? When I described him, Kurt said I could have just read the description on *his* driver's license and that he'd always had the feeling that he looked like his birth father.

Finding that baby/son/young man filled a hole in me that no person or material possession could ever fill. Since the day we made contact, my life quite simply has not been the same.

As painful as the separation from my son was, it was truly meant to be. I see reasons for this all the time.

I came here this lifetime to walk the path of my gifts. I would not have been able to accomplish all that I have if I had been a single parent. Also, as we've seen, I had a lot of wounds from childhood. These would have affected Kurt deeply if I had raised him. I had no self-worth for many years and would hate to have passed that on to him. If his father and I had tried to raise him together, I know I would have been in and out of a very codependent relationship. And, to be perfectly honest, I don't think I would have made a good mother. I was a "nervous Nelly," an alcoholic filled with anxiety and suffering from depression. None of that would have been good for my son.

Instead, Kurt was a wonderful gift for two loving parents. He has three brothers and a sister. He had a great life growing up in Lincoln, Nebraska, with healthy values and morals. He's now a husband and father of two — and one heck of a great guy. (You can see pictures of Kurt, my daughter-in-law, and my grandchildren on my website, www.echobodine.com.)

The timing of our meeting was perfect in that I was able to work on my issues *before* meeting him. I was able to bring a healthy person, rather than a dysfunctional one, into our relationship. God, in His infinite wisdom, knew when I was carrying that child that I would be a mom one day, but not until both of us were ready. While Kurt was growing up in his very cool family, I was on my own journey — growing, healing, and becoming a person who could be a good mom.

In this good, I find God.

PART THREE

Life Today

A MOVIE CAME OUT IN 1980 called *Resurrection*. It was about a spiritual healer, and I thought it was just great. I found it an accurate description of what it can be like to have the gift of healing. The healer in the film had faced quite a bit of resistance from the people in her community and eventually moved away. In the last scene, you see that she has bought a gas station. A family pulls in to get some gas, and it's obvious that the little boy has cancer. The healer puts her hands on him in an inconspicuous way and distracts him by showing him a dead two-headed snake displayed at the station.

When I saw *Resurrection*, I remember thinking that I would like to live that way with my gifts someday — not making a big deal out of them, not setting up appointments with people and charging money, just touching people when I was led to and channeling information to them when spirit spoke through me. That was almost thirty years ago, and I'm happy to say I've finally reached that place.

People still call for healings and readings. If I feel led to work with them, I do, but it's much different now. God guides me in all my work, and I spend most of my days in silence, listening for guidance. The level of energy that I can channel through my body has continued to increase over the years, and I now do healings on large groups of people. My psychic abilities have also continued to grow, although I now consider myself to be more of a spiritual teacher than a psychic or healer. I love teaching people about their own psychic and healing gifts. I believe this is my life's purpose now.

As ever, I've had some fascinating experiences during this stage of my journey. . . .

CHAPTER TWENTY-TWO

9/11

FOR THREE DAYS LEADING UP TO 9/11, I was antsy. Something was wrong somewhere, but I didn't know what it was. I also had a tremendous headache. It wouldn't budge, no matter how much ibuprofen I took.

The morning of 9/11, my phone rang early, but I had an inner sense not to answer it. I remember going to turn the radio on and my inner voice booming, "No!" The voice was pulling on me to pay attention only to it, so I did. It said no TV, no radio, no communication with anyone for a while.

I stayed in the silence that morning and afternoon, in spite of all the phone calls coming in.

I had a sense that I needed to feel my safety. It was an odd feeling and one that's hard to describe. It was like God was saying, "Focus on me and only me for now." I could see white light emanating from my solar plexus and surrounding my body. I stayed in that safe feeling until four o'clock that afternoon, when my inner voice told me to check my phone messages.

There were calls from several friends and from my family. There were also messages from radio stations asking if I would come that day to help people cope with what had happened. My friend Ginny keeps her television on CNN all day, so I knew she would know what was going on. She explained what had happened and told me to turn on my set. I had a very strong sense to do just the opposite. I needed to stay in a feeling of safety while I did the radio interviews. Then I could watch TV.

I called the radio shows and did the interviews. People were panicking, and I knew my job was to remind them that their inner voices would guide them if they were in an unsafe situation. People felt very victimized and needed to be reminded that they had their own inner knowingness that could keep them out of harm's way. They also needed to hear a calm voice. If I had been watching the airplanes going into the towers over and over on television all day, I would not have been able to bring people what they needed. I was grateful I had listened to my voice within.

I did turn on my television that night and watched for a long while. I felt the same feelings of powerlessness and grief that the rest of the country was feeling. It took discipline for me to get my focus back on the white light and not get caught up in the feelings of hopelessness, rage, and hatred that others were caught up in. I had to remind myself that God was in this experience, too. I knew it would take some time to see any good in it, but I tried to trust that it would be clear at some point.

By the next day, it was obvious that the events had brought people closer together. In the days and weeks following the tragedy, I saw people being kind to one another in big and little ways everywhere I looked. There seemed to be gentleness and consideration

as people went about their daily tasks. We had a perspective we
hadn't had before.

FOR YOU TO THINK ABOUT

Finding Calm in Crisis

I'd like you to spend some time journaling about all the
good you've seen come out of the experience of 9/11. Think
back to positive stories you read, to people you've talked to
and how it changed their lives for the better. This is an
important exercise because if and when something like this
happens again, we can immediately go to our journals and
remember the positive things that came out of a previous cat-
astrophe.

In difficult times we need reminders that life has not
completely fallen apart. We need to remember that the sun
will come up the next day and that we will continue on.

I would also like you to start spending quality time in
silence, possibly on a weekend when you have few commitments. Spend an hour in quiet — no radio, no TV, no emails.
Just be in your home or in nature, someplace where you can
simply *be*. You can do laundry, work on a hobby, clean the
house, go for a walk. But spend at least an hour of your time
alone with God — and keep your journal at hand for messages
you receive, pictures that pop into your mind, thoughts that
come into your head, inner nudges and knowings.

The more time you can spend in silence, the calmer you
will be when crisis strikes. Hopefully, when the next drama
comes, your first instinct will be to stay in the calmness of

silence rather than turning on the TV. We need to get grounded at these times. We need to feel safe and calm before diving into drama. We can do this if we discipline ourselves.

Please give silence a try. I think you'll be surprised at how nice it is not to hear all the commotion of the world.

CHAPTER TWENTY-THREE

Hospital Visit

ON A HOT DAY IN JUNE 2003, I was alone at my teaching center, setting up tables for a healing class that night. Suddenly I doubled over in pain. This feeling came on fast and out of nowhere. I couldn't stand up straight, and the pain was almost unbearable. I somehow made it to my car and though hunched over in pain, managed to drive home.

I literally felt like I was in labor. Because I had been hospitalized twice before with colon problems — that had led to surgeries — I was terrified. I did not want to go through any of that again.

When I got home, my boyfriend took one look at me and said that we needed to get to the hospital. All I could think about was the expense of spending ten days in the hospital and away from work. Remember that paying off my bills for previous hospitalizations had lost me my house. Even my inner voice was yelling, "Call an ambulance," but stubborn and afraid, I called my kinesiologist Marcie instead. I figured if she couldn't fix it, I'd go to the hospital. I was hoping against hope that the pain would just stop so that I could teach my class.

When Marcie arrived, she said I had an ischemic bowel and there was no time to waste. So just as my inner voice had said to do, I called an ambulance.

When I got to the hospital, they took X-rays, saw some kind of shadow on my intestines, and admitted me. I had no health insurance. All I could think was, "I can't afford this . . . ten days . . . must get back to work." I had clients and obligations; I did not want to be sick. Everyone tried to comfort me by saying that no one spends ten days in the hospital anymore, but I was fixated on that number.

The next morning, a woman from the hospital's financial office came in to talk to me about the bill. While she was in my room, I had a really bad attack of the pain. She told me she would do whatever she could to get me some assistance with the bills, and then she left.

There was a feeling in the room when she was there. From that day on, I was able to see the experience from a higher perspective. It was as if I was wrapped in a cocoon of protection. Even when I was in physical pain, I could rise above it, just watch it rather than feel it. When the nurses came in and poked me for blood, I could feel the needle, but it didn't hurt. When they wheeled me down for tests, it always felt like a group of angels was riding with me.

Toward the end of the second day, an angel that has worked with me for years, named Lilli, showed up. This was unusual because normally Lilli only came when I was doing readings or teaching classes. I asked her what was going on, and she gave me a "don't even *try* figuring this out" look.

Every morning I asked God to guide me that day. I spent a lot of time in silence (no TV or radio), just listening for guidance. Lilli would tell me when it was time to go for a walk and would go with me. She'd tell me to slow down near certain patients' rooms, and healing energy would come out of my hands. Sometimes I'd just stand in the doorway for maybe five seconds and say hello to the people in their rooms while the energy was coming out. I felt an interesting oneness with the other patients. I could feel a loving energy in my heart for everyone I came in contact with.

The nurses who cared for me all felt like angels. They knew my condition was a painful one and did so much to help me. I had a feeling of oneness with them as well; it was as if we were all connected, and this was very comforting.

One morning, while I was being wheeled down for a second colonoscopy, I was very tired and somewhat anxious about having to go through this again. The nurse assigned to me introduced herself and said that she had read all my books and loved my work. She could see that I was feeling stressed, so she snuggled me up in warm blankets and held my hand until they called my name.

On the fifth day, I got a roommate with a severe case of asthma. She was very anxious about being in the hospital and in between horrible, hacking coughs, talked constantly on her phone. Whenever she came over to my side of the room, my hands would heat up, and she'd calm down.

The next day I woke up to the sounds of a terrible coughing spell. I felt drawn to do something. Intuitively, I knew I was supposed to channel healing to her but wasn't sure if I should come out and tell her I was a channel or if the Universe would provide an opportunity.

Seconds later, my roommate came over and sat on my bed. It was obvious she was really hurting about something, and out of my mouth came the question, "Do you have children?" Then I reached over to touch her arm, and I could feel the healing energy flowing into her body. She told me about her son, who had been murdered a year earlier, and purged a lot of emotional pain in just ten minutes, sitting on my bed. Afterward, she went back to her bed and fell into a deep sleep. I also fell back to sleep. When I woke up, I wasn't sure if my experience with my roommate had been a dream or reality.

About five o'clock that day, Lilli and I went for an extra-long walk. When I came back to my room, my roommate was packing up to leave. Her vitals were normal, her X-rays were clear, and her fever was gone. She even looked like a different person. She had been carrying a great deal of grief in her lungs, and I believe she had finally released it.

On my walk with Lilli that day, I'd noticed that many of the rooms were empty. When I asked a nurse, "Where is everyone?" she said people were going home earlier than expected. I smiled.

One woman was there for several days. Whenever I walked by her room, my hands stopped channeling healing energy. I wondered why there was such a cold vibe around her room, so I opened up psychically and saw a very dark aura around her. This usually indicates impending death or depression. The next day there was a "code blue," and I later found that it was hers and that she'd died.

On the seventh day, I got a new roommate. She had received a kidney transplant, which her body was rejecting. I had a definite sense that I needed to touch her. I walked over to her bed, put my hand on her arm, and asked if she would like me to get her some iced tea downstairs when I went for my walk. She looked me in the eye and said she'd like to come with me. This was great because the whole way downstairs, I was able to keep my hand on her shoulder. I told her I needed to do this to steady myself.

When we got back to our room, we both took long naps. When I woke up several hours later, my roommate was dressed and ready to leave — they were sending her home. I heard her on the phone, arranging to be picked up by a relative. "I know, I can't believe it either," she said. Again, all I could do was look to God and smile.

On the eighth day, I could feel a shift taking place in my body. The doctors had done numerous tests, including two colonoscopies, and their final diagnosis was that the blood supply had been cut off to a part of my colon (ischemic bowel, as Marcie had predicted) and was healing itself. They wanted me to stay a few more days, and on the tenth day, my inner voice told me it was time to go home. We had accomplished what we'd come to do.

I had not wanted to be brought to the hospital, but now it was hard to say good-bye to everyone and leave that safe cocoon. I had even become friends with the people who cleaned my room. It was as if we were all on the same team — my uniform just looked different from theirs.

Everywhere I went, I was taken care of. So much took place over those ten days. When I came out of the hospital, I knew it was time to make some changes. I felt like I had moved to another level spiritually and also that I wouldn't understand all of it for weeks or months. But the level of closeness I felt to God was something I couldn't put into words. I really felt like He and I had walked hand in hand for the past ten days. I *loved* it.

Oh, yes, I almost forgot. Another miracle took place during my hospital stay: for some reason — still unknown to me — the county picked up the tab for my bill, something that had never happened to me before.

CHAPTER TWENTY-FOUR

The Boy in the Intersection

IN JULY 2005 I WAS IN LOS ANGELES auditioning for the part of teacher/housemother on a reality TV show. In my role, I'd be teaching a house full of people to develop their psychic abilities. Sounds fun, right?

I was excited, but I'd also been arguing with myself for weeks about whether to put myself through the meetings and audition process again. It wasn't the first time I had flown to LA to talk to television producers about being involved in one of their projects. I'd done this two or three times in the past, and someone else always got the part. (None of the shows ever took off.) It was actually at the urging of my inner voice that I booked a flight. I was more self-confident by this point and had a feeling that I was ready to handle whatever this job entailed.

The interview took place in the old Jim Henson Muppets studio, and just being there calmed me down. Statues and paintings of Miss Piggy, Kermit the Frog, and the rest of the Muppet gang lined the halls; I felt like a little kid.

The man who interviewed me was one of the executive producers of a very popular program. Aside from his being a skeptic, he was an absolute delight. After we chatted about the show, he told me he wanted to see me in action. He asked me to give him and the other folks in the room — two publicists, another producer, and his assistant — readings. The only times I remember being that nervous doing a reading for someone were when I read James Van Praagh and once when I was working in Malibu and my favorite movie star came in for a session with me.

I closed my eyes, took a big, deep breath, and asked one of the gentlemen to give me a question. And away I went. I gave each person a brief but significant reading (except for the assistant, who didn't want to be read in front of everyone), and when I opened my eyes, they were all sitting there with their mouths hanging open. The producer told me they had been interviewing psychics for months and that he was very impressed with my abilities. He stood up, extended his hand, and told me I had the job. I was on cloud nine and so grateful that I hadn't let my insecurities prevent me from flying out for the interview.

I had dinner plans with two dear friends that night, and my good news was going to make the evening even more special. My friends took me to a very nice restaurant on the corner of a busy intersection in Santa Monica. There was a huge picture window at the front of the restaurant. I was sitting with my back to this window when we heard a loud crash. My friends had looks of horror on their faces, and when I turned around, I saw that a car had collided with a motorcycle. A young man had gone flying into the air and crashed down into the intersection.

"What can I do?" I thought. "What *should* I do?" Before I could answer my own questions, my friend Victoria stood up, grabbed my hand, and said, "C'mon, you can fix this kid."

In our fancy clothes and high heels, we ran out of the restaurant, into the busy intersection, and over to the young man. A huge crowd had gathered and was hovering around him. Everyone seemed to be yelling. With all the confidence in the world, Victoria cut through it all, saying, "This woman is a spiritual healer and she can help him. Please move back."

One man in the crowed looked at me with such anger in his eyes. He told me not to touch the kid. But I felt so guided that nothing could have stopped me.

I sat down on the ground next to the boy and told him I was a spiritual healer. I asked him if it would be okay if I channeled healing energy to him. He very quietly said, "Yes." He was in a fetal position on his side and his breathing was hyper. I laid one hand on his chest and one on his hip. I then told him to focus on the calmness of the healing energy coming out of my hands. Within a minute, he was breathing normally. It felt as if he and I were the only two people in the world, even though we were right in the middle of a huge intersection, with lights, sounds, and people all around us. I felt like God had surrounded us in a protective bubble. I told him to forget about all the commotion and to just listen to my voice. I called him "Honey" and talked to him like a mother would talk to her injured child. I reassured him that the healing energy was going deep inside to heal his body and that I wanted him to focus on just the two of us. It was magical how everyone moved away and left us alone.

When the police arrived, a female officer came and asked if I was an EMT. I looked her in the eye and said, "No, I'm a spiritual healer." She smiled, nodded as if to say, "Carry on," and walked away.

Shortly afterward, the ambulance arrived, and I knew I had to leave the young man in the paramedics' care. As I walked away, they were cutting off his clothes, and I heard them say he had no broken bones and was not bleeding anywhere.

Victoria and I held hands as we walked across the street and back into the restaurant. When we joined our friend Marta, the three of us sat in silence for a few seconds. There weren't any words to describe what we were all feeling, and I was fighting back the tears of gratitude for being able to be a part of such an amazing experience.

The experiences I'd had earlier in the day, of meeting producers and agents, and talking about being on television, seemed insignificant now. I felt so close to God because of the work we had just done together. Later that night, as I lay my head down to go to sleep, I remembered having asked God earlier in the week, "If I get the television job, please don't let me forget my priorities." It was clear that He hadn't.

P.S. This television show didn't come together any more than the previous ones had. We prepared for it for months, but three days before taping was to begin, the network pulled the plug. It seems the point of my going to Los Angeles was not only to be on TV but also to be with the boy in the intersection.

CHAPTER TWENTY-FIVE

Healing Pen Pals

ABOUT SIX MONTHS AFTER THE INCIDENT with the young man in the intersection, I had a pretty serious health scare myself.

I was sitting in a restaurant with my boyfriend, just finishing dinner, when I got a very bad gripping pain on the right side of my head. I grabbed onto the table because the pain was so excruciating. My head suddenly felt disconnected from my body. My vision changed. I felt cut off from everything around me.

I opened my mouth to tell Mike that something was wrong, but my tongue felt so thick I couldn't get the words out. I pointed to my mouth and tried to speak, but the words came out so distorted that neither of us knew what I saying.

When I was finally able to say, "Something's wrong," Mike looked at me in the strangest way. Worry was written all over his face, which is uncommon for him. He told me to talk again, and in very slurred speech, I told him my tongue was too thick and I couldn't. I told him my head hurt "really bad."

We both knew something was very wrong when the waitress brought the check and I couldn't remember how to spell my name. I scribbled on the bill and almost started to cry. I couldn't read my own writing, couldn't remember how to spell "Echo." My head was a complete jumble of letters and words; nothing made sense.

Mike said he thought I was having a stroke, and when he said this, I knew he was right. But I just *could not* deal with it — sitting in the emergency room for hours, waiting for doctors to determine what was wrong, another hospitalization without insurance. I told Mike I just wanted to go home and get into bed. "I'll be fine," I said.

When I stood up to walk, my legs felt like they weren't mine. I could not walk a straight line. Mike put his arm around me and had to guide me to the car. The whole experience was surreal; I couldn't believe it was happening.

When I got home, I lay down on my bed, hoping against hope to fall asleep and wake up feeling normal. But I couldn't sleep. I knew something serious was happening to my body, even though I kept pretending it would pass.

I rationalized that it was all the stress I had been through with the cancellation of the reality TV show. Or perhaps my heavy schedule, teaching many classes every week and doing a radio show every Saturday night. I lay there trying to explain the whole experience away. But my brain was like scrambled eggs, and I couldn't make sense of anything. Still I told Mike to go home. "I'll be just fine," I said. "I just need some sleep." But shortly after he left, a voice whispered to me to call my doctor *now*.

When I called her, her associate told me that I showed every sign of having had a stroke. I needed to call an ambulance and get to a hospital immediately. I just lay there crying, still in disbelief that this was all happening to me.

I called Mike and asked him to come back. Then I called an ambulance, and within minutes, I was on my way to the hospital.

The doctors did feel that I'd had a stroke and admitted me to the neurological floor. There was a shadow on my CT scan that indicated something had happened, and I continued to speak as though I was drunk. I also walked like a toddler and kept running into walls.

When a woman from the speech therapy department came in to work with me, she showed me simple pictures and asked me what they were. When she showed me a picture of a hot dog, my head knew it was a hot dog but my mouth said, "Boat." Ketchup came out "flower." Cookie came out "bike." Staff asked me the same questions over and over, and I couldn't remember the answers. It was frightening and frustrating, and often, when it was all too much, I just cried.

Walking was such a challenge. When a physical therapist came in with a cane and told me she was going to teach me to walk with it, I just wanted to lie back down, close my eyes, and never wake up. I was too young for this! I had work to do. I had a radio show to get ready for. "Please, God, take this all away. Please heal me."

On my second day in the hospital, one of the nurses asked if I would like to see a healer from their alternative health care program. I was thrilled that they had such a program. Just hearing about it gave me hope. The healer came in that afternoon and worked on my head. The energy felt great, and I slept like a baby that night.

I was also receiving other healing. I have a program called the Healing Pen Pals consisting of more than a hundred students that I or my business partner, Carol Lowell, have trained. People from around the world email or write to us and request healing. The two coordinators of the program, Sybil and Cathy, then assign a healer to send absentee healing to each sick person every day for two to four weeks. We offer this service free of charge. All we ask is that people write us back and let us know how the sick person is doing.

As soon as I went to the hospital, my assistant sent the word out to Sybil. More than a hundred healers were now sending healing energy to me.

On my third day in the hospital, my doctor said that yes, I had had a stroke, but they were baffled by some of my blood work and other test results. Some indicated that *something* had happened to my brain, but other tests were inconclusive. He ordered a full panel of blood work, including something like ninety different tests. (But don't quote me on that number; my memory's a bit foggy on the whole thing!) When the tests came back a few days later, the only problem they could find was that my thyroid was low.

I saw the hospital's healer again on day three of my stay, and by day four, my speech was back to normal. I no longer needed a cane to walk, though I continued to veer off to the right for the next six months. And the pain in my head was decreasing by the day. Tests were coming back normal, the shadow in my brain scan was changing, and on day five, my doctor said, "Okay, now I don't know *what* you had, but I do know you can go home."

(This is very similar to what happened when I was hospitalized for the ischemic bowel I wrote about earlier. At the start of that hospitalization, my X-rays showed a shadow in the bowel, proof that something was amiss. But by the end of ten days, hardly anything was visible, leading the doctor to conclude that the bowel had "healed itself.")

I wish I'd had the presence of mind to tell the doctor about all the healing I was receiving. It didn't even occur to me, but that's probably for the best; he didn't seem the type who'd be open to such things. As a matter of fact, when he first came in to see me, he said, "So, you're a psychic, huh?" When I said that I was, he replied,

"Good. Tell me about my love life." My head was too muddled to be psychic, and that was the extent of our personal conversation. He was all business from there on out, never even making eye contact with me. It was odd, but then again, so is having a stroke!

They wanted to send me home with lots of pain pills for the headaches I was having, but I declined. They insisted I take steroid pills (for the rest of my life) so that I'd never get another migraine, even though they didn't know whether or not the migraines were connected to the stroke. But I literally heard my body say, "No way!" whenever I went to take one. She (my body) knew what was good for her, and this particular pill was not a good thing, no matter what I'd been told.

The healers in my network continued to send healing because I was still having some problems — daily headaches, which continued for months; walking to the right, which I still do when I'm overtired; and periods of what I call "blankness" in my brain, which forced me to take a three-month leave from my radio show and teaching. It was not the easiest of times.

I also had a few brief visits to the ER when I could feel my brain swelling. They would give me an injection of steroids, and the swelling would go down almost immediately.

It was quite a journey — not one I'd want to take again. But as always, I had God by my side. In spite of how things appeared on the outside, there was always a sense of calm deep inside.

I wrote this chapter so that you could see the power of prayer and healing. I'm so grateful to Abbott Northwestern Hospital for being advanced enough to offer an alternative health care program. And I'm ever so grateful to all the wonderful healers in the Healing Pen Pals program.

If you ever have a need for healing, please don't hesitate to contact us at Penpals@echobodine.com.

CHAPTER TWENTY-SIX

Road Rage

ONE EVENING MY ASSISTANT and I were driving back to my house after doing a book-signing at Barnes & Noble. We'd had a great turnout and were both in great moods, chatting away about anything and everything.

Suddenly, a car came around a curve in the lane coming toward us, going very fast. I had my high beams on, and I turned them off when I saw the fast car approaching. But when the car got closer, the driver was honking his horn and yelling obscenities about my "trying to blind him." I looked down and realized I had accidentally turned my bright lights back on. The angry driver thought it was intentional, when in reality, I had just been flustered by his reckless driving and angry energy. Every other word out of his mouth started with *f*, and he was driving so erratically, I suspected he was high on something.

The driver and his buddy finally drove out of sight, and Nancy and I continued on our way. But then, in the rearview mirror, I saw that the driver was backing up at a very high speed. I was only blocks from my home, so I sped up and then pulled into my driveway. My adrenaline was pumping now as I watched him back right up to my car. He had me completely blocked in.

Nancy begged me to stay in the car and call the police, but something very strange happened. A calmness came over me. I felt like I was floating on a cloud as I got out of my car and walked over to what I now saw were teenage boys — still yelling obscenities at me. As I walked, both my hands filled up with healing energy, and as soon as I reached their car, I reached inside and gently grabbed hold of the passenger's arm. In a very calm voice, I said to the driver, "Honey, what's wrong? Why are you so upset?" I visualized healing moving throughout the car. As I did this, the driver, who had seemed beside himself with rage, immediately calmed down. In a normal voice, he said that he thought I was trying to blind him. I calmly told him that I was very sorry. I'd gotten flustered by his anger and had accidentally turned my brights back on.

Heat was now pouring out of my hands, and I could see a change coming over the passenger. Within seconds, both of the boys apologized, telling me they were very sorry to have frightened me. I felt like I was outside my body, watching God take care of this explosive situation. I felt humbled by the experience as I watched the young men drive away. As they did, all three of us were *smiling* at each other. Only moments earlier, there had been only anger and fear between us.

Yes, I know things could have gone horribly wrong when I approached their car. But I'm confident that if they'd had a gun or other weapon, I would not have felt guided to approach them. I would not have felt safe and protected and so would not have done this. (I'm no daredevil!)

God was clearly in charge of this situation. I'm grateful I listened to my inner voice rather than the fearful voices in my head. If I had stayed stuck in my fear, and they in their anger, the situation could easily have escalated — and left none of us smiling.

FOR YOU TO THINK ABOUT

Don't Engage Rage

If you ever find yourself in a similar situation, my advice is very simple. If you are feeling any kind of rage, fear, and so on, don't engage in it.

If, on the other hand, you are getting "nudged" by calmness, let your internal spirit guide you — *but only if you are in the calmness.* As I described, in this instance I felt I was surrounded by a safe, white cloud of protection. It was my inner knowing that guided me to get out of the car and talk to the teenagers.

I've also been in rage-filled situations when even though my adrenaline wanted me to engage, my inner voice stepped in and said, "Stop!"

CHAPTER TWENTY-SEVEN

The Real Secret

GOD. A LITTLE, THREE-LETTER WORD that should bring comfort and calmness to all of us has so much negativity associated with it that it's no one wonder people are struggling to know if they can trust this God.

Insurance companies call catastrophes "Acts of God," so no matter how much we want to turn to this Supreme Being for help and comfort, we have these negative thoughts in the backs of our minds. These thoughts affect us, whether or not we're aware of them.

People blame God for everything, from war and losing loved ones to bad weather, the car breaking down, and getting laid off from their jobs. Deep down we seem to believe that anything negative that happens to us has come straight from God. This is such a shame because the single most important thing I've learned is that God does not create these things; we do. Our low self-worth, our expectations and beliefs, and our powerful thoughts and fears bring these things into our lives.

A book called *The Secret* came out in 2006 and was a huge hit. Its timing was perfect. People were searching for the next step on their evolutionary paths, and *The Secret* met that need. People formed groups and began visualizing all that they wanted to manifest in their lives, a bit like we did in my old Master Mind group. Oprah had the book's authors on her show, and a "*Secret* Movement" took off. It was good to see how excited people became when they realized how powerful their own thoughts are.

I enjoyed the book, and the DVD even more. Both were well put-together, and the message was important for people to hear. But I have one issue with the book's philosophy: it doesn't stress how important our self-worth is in manifesting our dreams. Our self-worth is the foundation of everything we do. If we have a healthy sense of self-worth, we lead healthy, productive, and abundant lives. We just naturally expect good things to happen to us.

On the other hand, people with low self-esteem are always struggling in one way or another. They don't feel *worthy* of having their life dreams fulfilled. They always expect "the other shoe to drop." Even if they were to win the lottery, they would live in fear that all the money would somehow disappear. A lack of worthiness affects every area of our lives, including our relationships with God. We think that if we don't win the lottery — or find the love of our life or get the perfect job — it's God punishing, judging, or keeping happiness from us. The truth is, it's our own fundamental feelings that can keep the good at arm's length.

We need to realize that before we can manifest what we visualize, we need to heal the old wounds and poor self-image that say we don't *deserve* to have what we want. In my life, there have been times when I did manifest what I wanted but then, because I didn't feel worthy of having it, found a way to sabotage it. When this happens, it's so easy either to blame God or to assume we have to visualize harder or pray louder.

What we really need to do is build our foundation. First and foremost, we have to feel worthy. We can't name and claim our dreams until we do.

One of the tough life lessons I watched my dad (and our whole family) go through was experiencing wealth. How can being rich be a tough life lesson? Let me show you what I mean.

Until I was fourteen, we lived in a modest home in a middle-income suburb of Minnesota. Dad was very hardworking and driven to succeed. He'd had a difficult upbringing, tossed from one foster home to another until finally being adopted, at age seven, by my strict, religious grandparents. He grew up during the Depression, so money was always tight. From all the bouncing around he did as a kid, he suffered from low self-esteem. Because he did little to recognize and heal it, his low self-worth affected everything in his life. To fight his fundamental feelings of unworthiness, he became determined to show the world he had a right to be here. He worked extremely hard, putting himself through school, getting a job at a company, and eventually buying that company.

Dad's company did so well that when I was fourteen, we moved from our modest home into a huge fourteen-room house in a wealthy suburb called Edina. Dad bought fancy cars for Mom and for himself. We had beautiful new furniture and could pretty much afford whatever we wanted. The first few years of this were fun, but after a while, we started to see another side of being wealthy. People we had never met would come to our house, or write Dad letters, asking for money. Dad would read us the letters and ask us who we thought money should go to.

Then there was the issue of wondering if people were our

friends because they liked us or because Dad was rich. This brought about a sad mistrust of people. When I entered college, I didn't tell people what high school I'd attended or anything else that might brand me a "rich kid." I wasn't being paranoid — the boy I became engaged to in college told me years later that he'd originally asked me out because he'd heard my dad was rich and that I would inherit his business.

Dad contributed large sums of money to charitable organizations and did a lot of community work. He was respected in the recovery community in part because he financially backed halfway houses in the Twin Cities area.

Despite all the good my father did and achieved, his low self-worth managed to undermine it. He could never really *feel* good about any of it. Instead of having a strong foundation of self-esteem, he tried to build a sense of worth based on how much he made, how much he gave to others, and how many material possessions he owned. But you can't build on a shaky foundation.

Eventually, the pressure of trying to keep all he'd built for himself became too much. He started taking Valium to relieve the stress, and this led to other drugs and alcohol. Over time, he lost everything. He filed for bankruptcy and left many people angry at him.

This was hard on the whole family. We all experienced the roller-coaster ride. We were raised with good values and morals, in a middle-class America where money wasn't the most important thing. Then we entered a new world in which wealth was every-thing. Then we lost it all.

Having gone through this, I never put winning the lottery on my list of life dreams! I'd much rather be in a partnership with God, knowing that whatever I need and want will be supplied, simply for the asking and for my highest good.

When we "do business" with God, when we are partners with God, we don't measure our worth by how much we earn, own, or even give away. We stand on much more solid ground. The secrets to building this kind of foundation are not mysterious:

- Get out of your head and into your heart. Head knowledge is no match for heart knowledge. Start listening to the still, small voice within. (Note: I don't mean to bash books; there are books — and tapes — some by me, some by others, that can help you learn to live by your inner voice.)

- Ask your inner voice to tell you what you need in order to have an amazing life. Then *listen*.

- Pay attention to the random thoughts, feelings, and images that pop into your mind throughout the day. This is part of listening.

- Ask your inner voice to show you what you need to heal your self-worth. Do what it says.

- Watch for so-called coincidences. Look at all the signs along your path and write about them in your journal. (Writing can really help us focus and become more aware.)

- Learn to bring your attention down to your gut. Get a sense of what it feels like when it says "yes" and "no."

- Talk to your inner knowing every day. God is not a trillion miles away, up above the sky. God is inside.

- After you've talked to Him, always give God the time and space to answer. Sit in silence, get on the treadmill, take a shower, keep the radio off in the car, go for a walk — whatever helps you to be quiet and focus on what's in you, rather than what's outside or around you.

- Don't worry about visualizing or praying the "right" way. When you connect, you'll know it — and you'll *love* it.

- Keep connecting. Keep the lines of communication open. Go to that internal voice first, for all your guidance.

As your self-worth is healing and you connect to the source that created you, trust that you are building the life of your dreams — on a solid, healthy, happy foundation.

There was a silver lining in my dad's experience. He eventually closed his business and did something he'd always wanted to do: he became a successful model in his fifties and sixties, and the experiences he had through that work deeply validated his self-worth. (See some photos of Dad on my website, www.echobodine.com.)

CHAPTER TWENTY-EIGHT

The New World
and the Beatitudes

THE MAYANS HAD A VERY PRECISE UNDERSTANDING of the solar system's cycles and believed that these cycles coincided with humanity's spiritual and collective consciousness. They prophesized that starting in 1999, we would have thirteen years to realize changes in our conscious attitude — to get off the path of self-destruction and move onto a path that opens our consciousness and integrates us with all that exists.

The Mayans said that seven years after the start of 1999, we would begin a time of darkness that would force us to confront our own conduct. This is the time when humankind enters the Sacred Hall of Mirrors. Here we look at ourselves and analyze our behaviors with ourselves, with others, with nature, and with the planet we live on.

As I write this book, there is a lot of buzz about the year 2012. People are asking me if the end of the world is coming and if so, how they should prepare.

Intuitively, I feel safe in saying that earth is not headed toward destruction but rather toward a new world. Take a look around at all that's going on. We see old ways breaking down while all that is necessary to usher in real change is emerging. We are more conscientious about the planet's environment than ever before. We're shifting our dependence on oil and finding solutions here in the United States. Through natural disasters, we're pulling together as a people rather than continually feeling separate from other countries and peoples. Our old health care system is breaking down, and it feels to me that by 2012, we'll have a revamped system. Top scientists are working on global warming, and we're going to continue to see more and more businesspeople, scientists, and politicians working together to find solutions.

I've seen a tremendous upswing in mental telepathy. People are communicating more and more with each other telepathically, and as we open up to the possibilities of this, our communication will be continuously shifting.

People's awareness of the deceased is ever increasing. People are no longer thinking of their loved ones who have passed as being somewhere far, far away. Increasing numbers of us are receptive to the possibility of communicating with them.

Technology continues to innovate and push the envelope at a rapid rate. In the next few years, we'll see those companies working to save or improve the planet succeeding in their efforts. Old business models that have sought only profit, and that have led to the depletion of resources and the destruction of the environment, will become obsolete.

Upcoming elections will put a different party in power, creating new pathways to 2012. (I get an image of Barack Obama riding a big wave on a surfboard. Choppy water is all around him, but he stays up on the board and has a smile on his face!)

Baby boomers will be working hard to change the way we treat the elderly. The economy is currently going through a Roto-Rooter detox, getting rid of the old bugs and making room for a new consciousness around prosperity. There are so many changes coming — and they're all good.

CONSCIOUSNESS IS SHIFTING RIGHT NOW

Two massive movements are taking place as I write, and they both have to do with Oprah Winfrey, bless her heart. One of the things I love about her is that she's not afraid of change, which is just what we need right now. She is someone we respect who continually introduces us to new ways of thinking and living.

Oprah is currently hosting an online class with Eckhart Tolle about his latest book, *A New Earth*. Last I heard, ten million people are tuning in every Monday evening to explore innovative ways of thinking and being. Ten million! If you stop to think about the fact that many of those ten million will share what they're learning with those around them, the potential impact of the class becomes mind-boggling.

Oprah has also just launched *The Big Give*, a television show about giving money to people in need and all that this entails. I love watching the show because it's so fun to see the choices people make.

I call both the class and the show "movements" because they are creating action around the world. I've seen several people in my own world inspired to figure out ways to give to others. It's very cool, and knowing Oprah, this is only the beginning. I'm grateful for this; we need people like her to blaze the trail and describe the path into the new world.

THE SECOND COMING

When I was preparing to write this chapter, I Googled "2012 the Mayan Calendar." I was surprised to find many sites proclaiming that the end of the world is coming, the Antichrist is on his way, terrorism is taking over the world, and so forth. There's little reason for this negative interpretation, and such a slant is extremely counterproductive. It's not that I think terrorists are suddenly going to say, "Oh, well, never mind," and pack up. But what I see is that eventually, as the consciousness continues to shift, darkness will not prevail.

Conversely, some people are saying that 2012 is when Jesus comes back to save us. I see the second coming idea in a different way. The movement I see in process has to do with people going within to become conscious of the Christ part of themselves. What's coming, what we now see happening, is a Christ Consciousness Movement.

Do you know that "Christ" is not Jesus's last name? Jesus's name is actually Rabbi Jeshua Ben Joseph, which means "Teacher Jesus, son of Joseph." Jesus's teachings are about us learning how to live the Christ way.

When someone says you are a "child of God," this means that you are unlimited potential. What does this mean?

I've talked repeatedly in this book about God being within you and about the still, small voice, or your intuition, as the voice of God. I'm hoping you now have a deeper understanding of what this means. I've seen students nod and give me a glazed look when I talk about this concept, so in case you've got that glazed look right now, I'm going to explain it with a metaphor.

Picture a peach. Now see the pit inside. That pit/seed produced the peach. But the peach never gives a thought to the seed that it came from. It looks around at the other peaches on the vine and thinks that's all there is, that nothing else exists.

We are the peach — and God is the seed. Many of us think of ourselves as having come only from our parents; we don't consider the original seed in our soul that created us. We assume what we're capable of doing and being by observing our parents and hearing stories about our relatives and ancestors. Like the peach, we look at the others around us and assume that's that — what we see is what it means to be human. We miss so much this way, not realizing that we are made from and of so much more. We don't think about divine potential. We don't understand what it means to be a child of God. We just go about our business, putting limitations on ourselves all the time and in every direction.

But then Jesus comes along. He says, "Hey everybody, God is within you, which means you are unlimited in what you can do. God loves you unconditionally. You don't have to prove yourselves — just strive to be the best you can be. You are gifted. You are amazing. Because you — yes, *you* — come from divine energy, intelligence, and light, you have potential to live up to." Jesus came here to set an example because we were stuck, thinking of ourselves as simple "peaches" without other possibilities.

THE CHRIST PART OF US

Jesus came to introduce us to the Christ part of ourselves. If you've ever read the Bible, you know we were in sore need of some good role models back then. Jesus came to be this kind of model. But He never wanted us to put the focus on Him. He came to serve as an *example*, and to show us something very important about ourselves.

How do we live from the Christ part of ourselves? Jesus laid it out for us in the Sermon on the Mount. He gave us eight Beatitudes to live by.

The problem with the Beatitudes is that we encounter them in an antiquated English that sends most of us into snore mode when we hear a sermon on them or read them in a book. *Blessed are they that mourn, blessed are the meek, for they shall inherit the earth* [try telling that to John Wayne!]. *Blessed are the poor in spirit, blessed are they that hunger and thirst,* and so on.

As I wrote earlier in this book, one of the spiritual texts my father gave me when I was fifteen was Emmet Fox's *Sermon on the Mount.* As you know, I loved that book. I knew intuitively that it contained the keys to living a good and fulfilled life, but because of its language, I wasn't certain how to interpret the Beatitudes.

It's only been by walking the path I've described in these pages that I've come to understand what they are saying. I'd like to look at each of the beatitudes, offer my thoughts on them, and then share them with you in my own words.

- Blessed are the poor in spirit; for theirs is the kingdom of heaven.

This one took me a while to understand, but it has to do with pride. Prideful people don't let God in. Their pride runs their life. So this Beatitude is saying blessed are the poor *in pride* because they are not above asking for help. They are not stuck in their egos so much that they see nothing but their own will. Blessed are the poor in spirit, for they are willing to open up to all that God has to offer them.

Do not let your pride run your life.

- Blessed are they that mourn; for they shall be comforted.

It's through our suffering that we come to know God. Unfortunately, most of us are stubborn. We don't embrace change unless it's forced on us. None of us wakes up when life is going great and says, "I think I'll go get on a spiritual path and find God." Difficulties prompt us to begin a spiritual search, and when we do, we find God. This opening allows us to be comforted by the presence of God. We search for God's voice and for God's answers. And we find them.

Don't keep anything buried inside. Keep yourself as emotionally clean on the inside as you keep your body on the outside.

• Blessed are the meek; for they shall inherit the Earth. This sounds like such a contradiction to most of us. We think of the meek as the guy who gets sand kicked in his face at the beach. But this is not the kind of meek Jesus is referring to. He is referring to the person who is humble. The Scripture that comes to mind is the one in which Jesus talks about his healing ministry and says, "It is not I, but the Father within me, that does the works." Life is a partnership with God, and those who acknowledge this, and know the truth about themselves — that they are cocreators with God — will inherit all that is.

Don't let your ego run the show.
Work on understanding your partnership with God.

• Blessed are those that hunger and thirst after righteousness; for they shall be filled.
How many times throughout this book have I mentioned my inner thirst to know God? When we have that thirst, we keep digging until we get to the truth about God: God is within us; we are one with God. And the more we meditate, the more we listen to that still,

small voice inside and feel our oneness with God, the more we are filled to the core of our being. Our thirst is quenched.

Recognize your internal thirst to know God,
and quench that thirst with meditation (listening to God)
and prayer (talking to God).

• Blessed are the merciful, for they shall obtain mercy. We hear versions of this Beatitude from many contemporary spiritual teachers. What we send out is what we get back. If we send out love, love comes back to us. If we are compassionate toward others, others are compassionate toward us. If we are patient with others, they will be patient with us. We get back exactly what we send out. It's another way of stating the Golden Rule: do unto others as you would have them do unto you.

Take charge of your happiness.
Only send out to others what you want to receive back.

• Blessed are the pure in heart; for they shall see God. This Beatitude is similar to the title of this book. Look for the good and you'll find God. If your heart is pure, you will only see the good, and when you see the good, you will see God. I think of my one-year-old granddaughter, who squeals with delight at everything in life. Her heart is pure, loving, and trusting. It never occurs to her to look for the bad. She is pure in heart and therefore trusting of all that is in her world. Jesus told us many times that we need to be like little children in order to enter the kingdom of heaven. He is talking about the trust little children have in their parents to fill their needs and wants. We need to be that way with our spiritual parent, knowing that all our needs and wants will be filled — simply because.

See God through the eyes of a child and learn to live
your life from that trust and simplicity
(what you send out comes back to you).

- Blessed are the peacemakers; for they shall be called
  Sons of God.

For some reason, I want to say this one backward. Blessed are the
Sons of God, for they shall be called peacemakers. A true son or
daughter of God seeks only peace. Jesus was all about working
things out peacefully — talking, reasoning, finding solutions. Jesus
was a peacemaker, not a warrior. It's always been so much easier
for men to pick up a club, a sword, or a gun and to try to create
peace that way. But that has only resulted in the deaths of so many
young men and women. When we truly know our oneness with
God and with each other, we will no longer go to war. We will
no longer see killing as a means to peace. We will no longer see
each other as enemies. We will instead work *peacefully* to achieve
peace.

Anytime you have a conflict, look at the solution
from the perspective of a peacemaker — no pride, no ego.
And apply the Golden Rule.

- Blessed are they that have been persecuted for righteousness' sake; for theirs is the kingdom of heaven.
  Blessed are you when men shall reproach you and per-
  secute you, and say all manner of evil against you
  falsely, for my sake. Rejoice and be exceedingly glad;
  for great is your reward in heaven; for so persecuted
  they the prophets that were before you.

This Beatitude has helped me more than any other in relation to people's criticism of my work and of the idea of living by intuition. Many people believe that living by the still, small voice within is irresponsible. My experience has been just the opposite. When we live by this guidance of God, we are on track 100 percent of the time. We are guided to make the wisest choices not only for ourselves but for everyone involved. This Beatitude clearly states that if we are following God, we should be exceedingly glad. Those of us on this path *are* exceedingly glad.

So let people have their opinions, but don't take them too seriously. If you are walking a spiritual path and are being fulfilled, if you know your oneness with God and live by the still, small voice within, by all means *rejoice*! Rejoice not only for all the rewards you're already experiencing but for having the courage — in the face of criticism, skepticism, and misunderstanding — to live by the messages given us by our brother Jesus.

What is most important is your relationship with God.
Don't let others tell you how to live or what you should believe.
Listen and live by the still, small voice,
and you will truly experience the magic of life.

In closing, I'd like to share one more personal story with you. It's about the Christ part of me.

Several years ago, my best friend called and asked me to please meet her at the hospital. Her twelve-year-old son had been in a skiing accident. She didn't have any details but had been told to meet the ambulance at the hospital.

On the drive over, I tried tuning in to the situation psychically and got a very somber sense. I wasn't sure how to interpret the feelings. As I was walking up to the hospital entrance, I asked God to be one with me and to work through me to do whatever was needed.

As soon as I stepped out of the elevator, I was met by a nurse telling me that my friend's son was virtually brain-dead. They needed my help to convince my friend of this because she couldn't or wouldn't hear what they were saying. From that moment on, I stepped into a place spiritually that I hadn't been in before. I had an inner strength and calmness that I'd never experienced. I knew God was working through me.

I went into the boy's room to communicate with his soul and find out what the plan was. I then had a vision of his soul on the other side and with his grandparents. They told me that he was going to stay there with them and that they would take good care of him.

My friend pleaded with me to channel healing to her son, but I could clearly see that he was not coming back into his body. Numerous decisions had to be made, and my friend asked me to take over and make them. Even though I had never been in a position like this, I was so connected to my inner knowing that the decisions were effortless.

The boy's father was on his way back from vacation in Mexico. We had no way of contacting him in these pre–cell phone days. No one was even sure what day he'd arrive. But at one point I had a vision of one of the airports here in the Twin Cities and heard a voice say, "Call right now and have him paged." I didn't even think about it but immediately picked up the phone and made the call. Lo and behold, within a few minutes, he was on the line. He was just walking out the front door of the airport when he heard himself being paged.

God worked through me every step of the way for the next week. I made clear decisions when the doctors needed an answer. I was with my friend constantly throughout a torturous week of making funeral arrangements and dealing with media coverage. (My friend was well known.) The funeral home called the night before visitation and asked me to come over and make sure the body looked right. Without flinching, I went, and in that very calm state, fussed with him a bit so that he looked perfect. I made it through the whole week on very little sleep. I was in a magical zone.

People commented that I had a light around me and that they felt very comforted by my calmness. When there was any kind of turmoil, I was guided to go stand in the middle of it, and the tension would dissolve.

I felt enormous gratitude to be part of this process. It's not that I was grateful for my composure or ability to act. And I was certainly not "grateful" for the pain and suffering all around me. What I was grateful for was the experience of the Christ within me, for feeling God literally working through me around the clock for an entire week.

I share this story because I want you to know that you have that same light and presence within you that I had and that Jesus has.

This is the way Jesus lived his entire adulthood. He lived in that magical zone, that God place, always expressing God, constantly working in partnership with God, continuously being guided by the still, small voice within.

This is what being on a spiritual path is all about — living *this* way of life, living the Beatitudes, living in conscious partnership with God, 24/7.

Each morning when you get up, ask God to help you live from the Christ part of you. At night, write about your day in your journal, because as you ask God for this help, you'll have a lot to write about. Pay attention, and I predict you'll be amazed by how you feel: grand, humble, excited, at peace, in the moment, powerful, playful, and courageous. When we consciously live from the Christ self within us, we create *a new world* to live in. We begin, as Scripture says, to have heaven on earth.

It all begins by looking for God in every experience. Do this, and you can't help but see the good.

Acknowledgments

EVERY ONE OF THESE CHAPTERS MENTIONS wonderful people I am deeply grateful to for being teachers, healers, or dear friends on my journey to knowing God. As you read the stories, you'll know who you are, and I thank you from the bottom of my heart.

My thanks also go to:

Georgia Hughes, for believing in this book and saying yes to publishing it, for being incredibly patient with me through my writer's blocks, for all the guidance you've given me in writing this, and for all the fun back-and-forth emails. You are the best, Georgia, and I love you dearly.

Yvette Bozzini, for all your expert help with editing. Once we found our groove working together, we had a lot of fun creating this book.

Kristen Cashman, for your final touches. You have an amazing eye for detail, and I greatly appreciate it. Kim Corbin, for all your great work promoting the book, and Tracy Pitts, for a beautiful cover.

And my wonderful webmaster, Chris LaFontaine, for creating a beautiful album of pictures for the book (on www.echobodine.com).

About the Author

ECHO BODINE IS A RENOWNED SPIRITUAL HEALER, psychic, and teacher. She has written nine books, including *Echoes of the Soul, The Key, Hands That Heal, The Gift,* and *A Still, Small Voice.* She lectures throughout the country on intuition, spiritual healing, life, death, and life after death. She also offers workshops through The Center, her teaching and healing center in Minneapolis, Minnesota. She can be reached at:

echo@echobodine.com

or

P.O. Box 19488
Minneapolis, MN 55419

NEW WORLD LIBRARY is dedicated to publishing books and other media that inspire and challenge us to improve the quality of our lives and the world.

We are a socially and environmentally aware company, and we strive to embody the ideals presented in our publications. We recognize that we have an ethical responsibility to our customers, our staff members, and our planet.

We serve our customers by creating the finest publications possible on personal growth, creativity, spirituality, wellness, and other areas of emerging importance. We serve New World Library employees with generous benefits, significant profit sharing, and constant encouragement to pursue their most expansive dreams.

As a member of the Green Press Initiative, we print an increasing number of books with soy-based ink on 100 percent postconsumer-waste recycled paper. Also, we power our offices with solar energy and contribute to nonprofit organizations working to make the world a better place for us all.

Our products are available
in bookstores everywhere.
For our catalog, please contact:

New World Library
14 Pamaron Way
Novato, California 94949

Phone: 415-884-2100 or 800-972-6657
Catalog requests: Ext. 50
Orders: Ext. 52
Fax: 415-884-2199
Email: escort@newworldlibrary.com

To subscribe to our electronic newsletter, visit
www.newworldlibrary.com